A
More
Just
Future

Also by Dolly Chugh

The Person You Mean to Be

A
More
Just
Future

Psychological Tools for Reckoning
with Our Past and Driving Social Change

Dolly Chugh

ATRIA BOOKS

New York   London   Toronto   Sydney   New Delhi

ATRIA
BOOKS

An Imprint of Simon & Schuster, Inc.
1230 Avenue of the Americas
New York, NY 10020

First Atria Books hardcover edition October 2022

ATRIA BOOKS and colophon are trademarks of Simon & Schuster, Inc.

For information about special discounts for bulk purchases, please contact Simon & Schuster Special Sales at 1-866-506-1949 or business@simonandschuster.com.

The Simon & Schuster Speakers Bureau can bring authors to your live event. For more information, or to book an event, contact the Simon & Schuster Speakers Bureau at 1-866-248-3049 or visit our website at www.simonspeakers.com.

Interior design by Jill Putorti

Manufactured in China

1 3 5 7 9 10 8 6 4 2

Library of Congress Cataloging-in-Publication Data
Names: Chugh, Dolly, author.
Title: A more just future : psychological tools for reckoning with our past and driving social change / Dolly Chugh.
Description: First Atria books hardcover edition. | New York : Atria Books, 2022. | Includes bibliographical references and index.
Identifiers: LCCN 2022004263 (print) | LCCN 2022004264 (ebook) | ISBN 9781982157609 (hardcover) | ISBN 9781982157623 (ebook)
Subjects: LCSH: Social change. | History—Study and teaching. | Resilience (Personality trait) | Racial justice.
Classification: LCC HM831 .C497 2022 (print) | LCC HM831 (ebook) | DDC 303.4—dc23/eng/20220128
LC record available at https://lccn.loc.gov/2022004263
LC ebook record available at https://lccn.loc.gov/20220042 . . .

ISBN 978-1-9821-5760-9
ISBN 978-1-9821-5762-3 (ebook)

For my parents

Contents

A
More
Just
Future

Prologue

So Much to (Un)Learn

In 2011, I read the entire Little House on the Prairie series aloud to my daughters. I loved sharing stories of this quintessential American family. We related so much to the Ingalls family that my husband and I devoted a weeklong summer road trip with our children through South Dakota and Minnesota, visiting the towns of Walnut Grove and DeSmet. We walked on the same soil, saw the same sky, and breathed the same American spirit as the family with whom we identified. Throughout the week, I found myself humming, *This land is your land, this land is my land.*

As the children of immigrants, we loved immersing our kids in this deeply American story. The vacation delighted our children, spared our budget, and glorified the patriotic values of hard work, family, and love of country that we emphasize in our home and nation.

A parenting triple play. Nailed it, I remember thinking, with a non-trivial bit of smugness.

Years later, I realized what a disservice I had done my children and the country I love.

Little House

If you have seen the television show *Little House on the Prairie,* you might remember the iconic opening, with the Ingalls girls in prairie dresses running through tall grass and wildflowers. At the time of our trip, our kids knew the books but had never seen the show from the 1970s and '80s. In a general store in South Dakota, we bought them prairie dresses, handmade by a local resident, because . . . cuteness. Later that day, with no parental prompting from us, the kids spontaneously reenacted that iconic scene and in a parenting miracle, we managed to snap a photo (finding that picture now is another story). Prairie dresses, tall grasses, flowing tresses . . . how I savored the sweetness of that moment.

Now I recall that trip with sweet nostalgia and sweet regret. The opportunity was literally in my lap to help my kids learn about our country's past, its beauty *and* its burdens. I missed the chance because I was thinking about Ma, Pa, Mary, Laura, and baby Carrie, not about their historical context.

So I doubt I paused to explain or consider that the Ingalls family built a house in "Indian country" because, as Pa explained to Laura, "When white settlers come into a country, the Indians have to move on." I likely tsk-tsked at racist phrases like "the only good Indian is a dead Indian," yet overall, I never questioned who the heroes—and villains—were in the American story I had grown up reading and watching.

I am no history buff, but I could have asked basic questions. Whose land did that little house sit on? How did Laura's family justify stealing land from the Osage Indians? Where did those Native Americans go? These questions pinched my thoughts every now and then, but I ignored them because I lacked the tools to engage the contradictions that surfaced or to untangle complicated narratives. I let my kids believe the same fables I had grown up believing.

I Wish

Looking back now, I wish I had seized the chance to help my kids learn age-appropriate truths. I wish I had named and embraced the paradox of the Ingallses as American heroes *and* colonizers. I wish I had connected the dots between events of Laura's time and events of my children's time. I wish I had rejected those fables of who the bad guys were. I wish I had helped my kids see that the Ingallses were good people benefiting from an unjust system that favored them and generations to come. Instead, I was burdening my kids with the same need to unlearn that I (and most Americans) carry.

In the United States, my generation and the one that raised us grew up playing cowboys and Indians and watching Westerns starring Roy Rogers, Gene Autry, and the Lone Ranger as heroic cowboys, civilized heroes conquering uncivilized savages. While my kids are less exposed to such games and movies, they are growing up at a time when tens of thousands of fans of the 2021 World Series champions Atlanta Braves do "tomahawk chops" with their phone flashlights in a stadium where the lights are deliberately darkened for maximal visual effect.[1]

In fact, Native American mascots for sports teams proliferate at professional, college, and K–12 levels, with many teams and fans claiming these symbols as signs of honor and respect. This argument is countered by the stereotypical, misleading, and insulting images of these mascots. The American Psychological Association recommends such mascot usage be retired because of the demonstrable harm it does to Native people it claims to represent and to non-Native people who absorb racist stereotypes.[2] The National Congress of American Indians argues that views of Indians as uncivilized were the premise of forced assimilation and genocide.[3]

And it is not just mascots. A *New York Times* teacher's resource titled "Teaching About the Native American Fight for Representation, Repatriation, and Recognition" highlighted the many ways—from TV shows to historical markers to return of artifacts—that Native Americans are fighting for social change.[4] I am struck by how few of these issues ever dawned on me. None of the systems of education or media or law that I navigate highlight these issues. When it comes to this history, there is much for me—and my children—to unlearn.

Good Guys Win

Granted, in 2011 when we took that trip, our country had serious problems but little idea of the despair to come. Trayvon Martin and George Floyd were alive. Barack Obama was president. Donald Trump was hosting *Celebrity Apprentice,* which Arsenio Hall would soon win. We had already forgotten the H1N1 swine flu epidemic of two years earlier.

I guess I wanted to believe that things were okay the way they were. Research by psychologist John Jost and colleagues shows that we tend to be invested in the way things are, albeit often on an unconscious level.[5] I like to oversimplify the "system justification theory" as the "good-guys-win mindset." The world, with its tomahawks and mascots, is filled with indefensible systems. Still, we are wired to see those systems and the world, including the past and present treatment of Native Americans, as good, fair, legitimate, and desirable. Good guys win. Even when the status quo harms our own interests, we are often inclined to defend that status quo. Something about that status quo addresses our underlying psychological needs.

One manifestation of this psychology is a colonial mentality in which we exalt white cultural values, behaviors, norms, and appearances at the expense of those of nonwhite people. Of course, there is much to admire in these values, behaviors, norms, and appearances; it is the exalting at the expense of nonwhite elements that make a colonized mind. Decolonizing one's mind is a process of untangling the systems that our mind has justified, especially when those systems do not serve us. In other words, to decolonize is to unlearn.

Accidental History Lessons

I did little to decolonize this (my) mindset as my children sat in my lap, begging for one more chapter. In my weak defense, we wanted the Ingalls sisters' story, not a history lesson. Nonetheless, bedtime stories often serve as accidental history lessons and you can be sure that I awarded myself parenting points for sprinkling in educational content at bedtime.

Accidental history lessons are everywhere. My kids (and everyone else) have been flooded with historical narratives since birth. Family members recount stories of their youth. Preschool teachers dress them up in bonnets for the olden-days show and tricorner hats for founding fathers' birthdays. Field trips and family vacations offer reenactments and restorations and Rushmores. Movies and TV shows transport them to the time of dinosaurs, wars, and old-fashioned chores. Statues and monuments stand tall in their parks, post offices, and police stations. Neighborhood kids still play the roles of soldiers and cowboys fighting enemies and Indians.

Even if reading to my kids at bedtime was more about the story than the history, our vacation was supposed to be different. Once we started driving our rental car around Minnesota and South Dakota, we were searching for context and the history. That was the point of the trip, to immerse ourselves in another world and another era. Our itinerary consisted of time travel.

Still, if I'm honest, I wanted to see the Ingallses' story through the eyes and memories of a child recalling her lovely, hardworking parents. I did not know how to honor the Ingallses *and* honor those they displaced. So I let those unsettling realities float away in the blue prairie sky. The question was not whether my kids were ready to face difficult questions of the past. The question was whether *I was.*

Not-So-Current Events

I have been thinking about that question a lot in recent years. Our national news cycle has become flooded with stories about the past. Many of us are learning aspects of American history for the first time. We are learning about the massacre in Tulsa, Oklahoma. We are learning about Juneteenth. We are learning about the abuse and killing of Native American children in compulsory "boarding schools" designed to destroy their culture. We are learning about the incarceration of Japanese-Americans. We are learning about the genocide perpetuated by the man on our twenty-dollar bill. We are learning about the brutal legacy represented by Columbus Day. We are learning who erected the Confederate monuments and why.

The stories keep coming, every day. It is hard to keep up with all of the history in the last paragraph, let alone in the news. With each story, we are flooded with guilt, shame, disbelief, and confusion. Did this really happen? How could it happen? And if it happened, how did I not know?

These news stories barely appeared in mainstream media—let alone in our headlines—until recently. Now we seem to have an unprecedented interest in unpacking our past. These stories are unearthing horrific truths we may not have known or assumed to be outliers. In the past few years, "current events" feel more like "historical events."

I noticed this phenomenon after my first book was published in 2018. I was eager to write another book, but my ideas were scattered. As with my first book, I wanted to use my expertise as a psychologist to tackle a moral issue that I was grappling with. To brainstorm, I decided to track ideas and headlines that grabbed my attention. I scribbled ideas on sticky notes and printed articles that made me stop scrolling long enough to read, piling them in a corner on my desk. My paper mountain grew by the day.

After a few months, I excavated the mountain, sorting by topic. Two things surprised me. First, almost every day, there was a headline about the past. By "about the past," I mean revelations about a time period typically covered in an American history textbook. These stories included unearthing buried ancestral grounds under a parking lot, a revelation that a seminary sold enslaved people to raise funds, and multiple controversies over words, monuments, people, logos, or flags associated with slavery.

Second, the pile of history-laden headlines was my biggest pile. How strange, I thought, as I do not even know if I get the History Channel. History is not really my thing. Nonetheless, I was struggling with the narratives I had long embraced about America as the greatest country on earth.

Reckoning with a Whitewashed Past

I suspect that I am not alone. Perhaps you are also feeling nudged for a variety of reasons, including: the rise of social media and the range of voices and traumas to which we are bearing witness; the unnerving realization of what did and did not make America great in the eyes of the forty-fifth president; and backlash against an election system that ignores the popular vote. In the racial justice sphere, the Black Lives Matter movement and the murder of George Floyd have illuminated issues that are neither new nor anomalous, revealing racial fault lines that the pandemic made undeniable. During the pandemic, we are seeing the effects of centuries of medical harm done to people of color, rippling into distrust in the national campaign to roll out factual information and lifesaving vaccines. In Charlottesville, Virginia, unmasked white supremacists were willing to kill to protect a symbol of hate that many people believed was a thing of the past. And across the nation, an obscure branch of legal scholarship called critical race theory has become the center of a bitter debate on how—and what—kids should learn about history in school.

These instances have something in common: a reckoning with a whitewashed version of history. In the whitewashed version of history, systems are justified and good guys win. When we whitewash the past, we "portray the past in a way that increases the prominence, relevance, or impact of white people and minimizes or misrepresents that of non-white people."[6] Again, we hear elements of a colonized mind.

Maybe we were never quite the ideal country we wanted to be, but we are less naïve than we were just a few years ago. This moment feels distinctive and critical. Call it a perfect historical storm. Many of us have been raising awareness in ourselves and others. We have been examining ourselves and interrogating our systems. We have been pushing for change and pulling for champions. Our present is reckoning with our past.

Our bookshelves reflect this moment. Many historians, writers, journalists, and storytellers are bringing us content that challenges the whitewashed narratives we have learned. Forty-plus years after the controversial publication of *A People's History of the United States,* by Howard Zinn, truth-telling books topping the bestseller and best-of lists include *On Juneteenth,* by Annette Gordon-Reed; The *Warmth of Other Suns* and *Caste,* by Isabel Wilkerson; *Between the World and Me* and *Eight Years in Power,* by Ta-Nehisi Coates; *Four Hundred Souls,* edited by Ibram X. Kendi and Keisha N. Blain; *How the Word Is Passed,* by Clint Smith; *The Sum of Us,* by Heather McGhee; *The 1619 Project,* created by Nikole Hannah-Jones; and so many more. My shelf runneth over.

Still, reading important books is not enough. I am still left with the ominous emotions of guilt and shame, dissuading me from connecting dots and embracing contradictions, not just intellectually but emotionally. These books offer us stormy emotional truths that we need to prepare for, as we would prepare for stormy weather. They push us to decolonize our minds. These books challenge us to reckon with a whitewashed past.

When I hear the word *reckoning,* as we have a great deal recently, I see a godlike person in robes passing ultimate judgment on mere mortals. I hear a booming voice pronouncing who is worthy and who will be sent away. Reckonings are lofty and large. So, I was surprised when I looked up the word. One dictionary defines *reckoning* as "the action or process of calculating or estimating something" or the "settlement of accounts as between two companies" or "a statement of an amount due; bill." These definitions evoked "accountant" more than "robed god."

This version of reckoning is important and useful. It suggests we need to get our records straight, balance our checkbook, and clean up our files. We need to calculate the cost of those takeout meals. We need to know how much money is actually in our savings account, not how much we wish we saved. If we live in white neighborhoods or work on white teams or socialize with white circles of friends, it means examining how that came to be rather than accepting that it just is. It means reckoning with our past and its presence in our present. It means reckoning with how individual actions, biases, stereotypes, and Karens are fueling (and are fueled by) systems of racism.

But *how* do we reckon? How do we discern and undo the link between the actions of our ancestors, our actions today, and the future actions of our descendants? It is going to require a different mindset.

A Child's Eyes

So here we are, unable to ignore our country's whitewashed past if we want to act in good faith as Americans who care for each other's unique and shared plights. At the same time, here we are, unable to face our past, which can be jagged and ugly. We are gasping at the gap between our ideals and our realities. We are exhausted with bad news in the present, never mind bad news from the past.

I wish we could just move on. With hopes as big as a prairie, I wish that a strictly forward-looking path would work. I want the solution to be as simple as unity and optimism. I want patriotism to prevail. I want to fly the biggest American flag in town and for that to be enough. I want us to stand united so that united we stand. I want to move forward. I want us all to agree on more things and fight about fewer things. I wish we got along better and felt less divided from each other along racial and ideological lines. I wish, I wish, I wish.

This yearning makes me crave the apparent simplicity of a child's world. Sit at the kids' table, where you can say what you want, believe in kids' stories, and tell kid jokes where the punch line is simple and free of nuance. I am lost in what psychologists call magical thinking, a need to believe that our hopes and desires can manifest in reality, without any action.[7] I do this often, when I create an impossible to-do list for a weekend (for example, "organize entire house") or comfort myself that my children will be free from harm as long as I know where they are (alas, if only). Childlike magical thinking often manifests for adults in times of stress.[8] But no amount of magical thinking, lucky numbers, and knocking on wood will address the challenges we face today. While magical thinking is cute in kids, we are not kids. We may reminisce about childhood, but most of us like the agency and independence of adulthood, not to mention the greater clarity about the world and the ability to understand what the grown-ups are talking about.

As a nonconfrontational scaredy-cat, I am drawn to the comfort of a time and society that felt less divisive and more united, if there ever was such a time, even in my child's mind.

But now I am also an adult more willing to sacrifice comfort in the present to pursue a more just future. At this distinctive moment, I appreciate the value of divisiveness, not because I want discord, but because unity is not the same as progress. The Civil War was divisive. The civil rights movement was divisive. Some people pushed for change and other people pushed back hard. Without the divisive times in our country's history, we would still be "united" in slavery and segregation. Divisiveness is not always bad.

Our time for being adults is now. To wish for a system to change on its own while we close our eyes is magical thinking. Our challenges today began centuries ago and the damage has deepened and widened over time. To take the path to a more just future, we bear witness to the damage through others' eyes and uncover its origins. We need—we want—to let go of children's stories and move to the adult table. There we are better able to question our ancestors, the very people whose stories we love to tell and in whom we take such pride.

A Story Both Right and Wrong

My friend Jeff Wilser wrote a book called *The Good News About What's Bad for You . . . and the Bad News About What's Good for You.*[9] I loved the concept. The title on the cover read "The Good News About What's Bad for You." But when you flipped the book upside down and over, you discover a second "front cover," which announced a rearranged title "The Bad News About What's Good for You." The book's contents were also split, with half of the pages focusing on things like the upside of eating Oreos (fun fact: Jeff went on a junk-food-only diet for thirty days; I am clearly doing this author thing all wrong) and the other half on the downside of eating kale (a less interesting challenge). Based on the science (and Jeff's lifestyle experiments), both things were true (to an extent).

I imagine a two-sided book about American history titled "What We Learned Was Right . . . and What We Learned Was Wrong." One side of the book would describe how people escaping religious persecution fled their homeland, leaving behind loved ones to travel in dank, dangerous conditions on a ship across a massive ocean. It would catalog how they struggled to survive disease and starvation, and the despair of losing so many fellow travelers on the ship before the multi-month journey ended on the shores of what they named Plymouth Rock. It would tell of a brutal winter and minimal food. It would capture the determination such a journey and such a winter must have required. It would relay how they overthrew a monarchy. It would describe how they built lives, families, colonies, democracy, and a capitalist empire in this new land.

This story is the equivalent of your high school basketball team beating an NBA team. They practiced hard, played hard, and never gave up. They never should have won. It's David beating a team of Goliaths, an awe-inspiring story of heroes, a fabulous and true story.

Then flip the book over, and the story would go differently. Those travelers followed the lead of someone who got lost and stumbled upon lands of millions of indigenous people. They invaded these communities; they destroyed systems of "commerce, travel, economies, permanency, stewardship, inheritances, artistry, drama, ceremony, mourning, health care, politics, justice, penance, peacekeeping," as a popular meme explains. One study estimates that between Columbus's arrival in North America in 1492 and 1600, violence and disease killed 90 percent of the indigenous population, plunging the population from 60 million to 6 million.[10] The population decline of 54 million people was so sudden and stark that it actually led to a global cooling trend referred to as the "Little Ice Age," as vegetation and farmland were untended, shifting the carbon dioxide absorption and greenhouse gas removal from the air. It is difficult to describe these dramatic events as anything other than slaughter and even genocide.

These invaders also stole millions of acres of land and millennia of culture from these indigenous peoples. As far back as the 1600s[11] and as recently as the 1950s, they removed hundreds of thousands of Native children from their parents' homes and forced them to attend "boarding schools" where they were forbidden to speak their native language or see their parents. The children who survived are still alive, now the same age as my parents.

What we learned was right. Except what we learned was also wrong, because it is also true that the "winners" played dirty. They doctored the clock and scoreboard. They lowered their basket while raising the other team's. They hard-fouled to injure. They bribed the refs. And, when they were declared victors, they published an article in the school paper belittling their opponents.

As the season continued, that team kept playing the same way, but got better at concealment. They got caught less. Their fouls were less flagrant and from a distance, many may have perceived a fair game. Many even believed things were fair, because good guys win. They played to weaken the other team's bench and souls, and then they said, "See, they don't play as hard as us so they don't deserve as much as we do." They declared victory while brandishing the sportsmanship trophy they awarded themselves.

Rub you the wrong way? Me, too. My system-justifying good-guys-win mindset is on red alert. Nothing is more American than the values of hard work and fairness. I struggle to reconcile that what we learned was right *and* wrong. My mind wants me to pick a side. My heart wants the less awful story to be the only true one. My soul needs it to be. Yet, American history is not that neat.

"I Didn't Have to Unlearn It"

Many of us, including me, were adults when we learned—or at least, registered—that the founding fathers enslaved other human beings. Michael Harriot, senior writer at *The Root,* was an adult when he learned that about the rest of us. As a black child homeschooled until age thirteen, Michael didn't know what *we* didn't know. Michael's family purposefully tried to raise kids "that weren't affected by white supremacy."

For example, perhaps we learned the following about slavery, women's suffrage, and World War II: white people freed the slaves; women got the right to vote; the Greatest Generation defeated the Nazis.

Michael shared his take in a *Root* piece titled "Y'all Tired Yet?": "They [America] became one of the strongest economies in the world because of our free labor and repaid us with a terrorist campaign called Reconstruction and Jim Crow. White women got the right to vote partly because of black women but said 'fuck y'all.' Black men fought in the first World War and got the lynching epidemic of Red Summer as a lovely parting gift. After World War II, they stole black veterans' GI benefits."[12]

If you are like me, you cringed when reading that paragraph. Maybe you were confused. Maybe you resisted. Maybe you dismissed. Maybe you argued. Maybe you looked up a few things. I did all of the above.

But when I reread the paragraph, I realized that none of it was untrue. Intellectually, I understand I need to unlearn and relearn a massive amount of history, but I don't know how to do this emotionally and psychologically.

I reached out to Michael for his take. As an African-American writer, spoken-word poet, and podcaster, Michael often writes about the white supremacy invisible to so many Americans. By phone, he explained, "If you have always been taught since you were five years old one version of American history that is a whitewashed or false version, then you will push back on any notion that dismisses the thing that you were taught. [It's like admitting] that you are wrong most of your life and acknowledging the very real possibility that you have been complicit. And people just don't like to feel guilty." Unlearning is not just intellectual work; it is emotional work.

"I didn't have to unlearn it," explains Michael. He can pinpoint the costs of not unlearning. "People don't see why things are the way they are. So they don't understand. If you don't know the history of redlining, if you don't know the history of segregation, if you don't know the history of how schools are funded, then you're more susceptible to those notions of white supremacy where black people are not as smart or don't work as hard because you don't know your history."

And when he says "your" history, he doesn't mean black people knowing the history of black people. Michael reflects: "We separate white American history and black history. There's black history and then there's American history. It's not the true reality of America. American history is, in part, black history, and the two are intertwined." To illustrate, Michael notes how Black History Month is often taught separately from American history. Why would white history be prioritized over another's?

As I speak with Michael on the phone, I recall the "Be Like Mike" Gatorade campaign from the 1990s. Forget Michael Jordan. I want to be like Michael Harriot. I want to see things as they are, not as I wish they were. I want to be intellectually honest and emotionally strong. Michael has less to unlearn than most of us. It is time we learned how to unlearn, and we'll need not only our heads, but our hearts and souls.

Lifelong (Un)Learners

In his book *Think Again: The Power of Knowing What You Don't Know,* organizational psychologist Adam Grant notes that we think "too much like preachers defending our sacred beliefs, prosecutors proving the other side wrong, and politicians campaigning for approval—and too little like scientists searching for truth."[13] Scientists are always testing hypotheses, collecting more data, making discoveries, rejecting faulty theories—all in search of the truth. In other words, scientists are always learning and unlearning.

We often hear about the value of lifelong learning. We hear less about the value of lifelong unlearning. If we're constantly learning, surely we need to amend earlier lessons. Some knowledge was never true, like the story of Thanksgiving. Some knowledge is true, but incomplete, such as the ideals of our founding fathers. Unlearning does not necessarily mean total erasure. It may be more of a loosening, where we hold less tightly to a single narrative. Or we may realize that some knowledge was once true, but is now obsolete.

The longer we have held knowledge and the more invested we are in that knowledge, the tougher it will be to unlearn.[14] So we will need to be patient with ourselves. We did not learn these narratives instantly and we cannot unlearn them instantly.

Consider when we say "we are a nation of immigrants." This narrative feels true. It matches our vision and our aspiration of ourselves as a people. It speaks to our pride in our heritage and our lineage. Unfortunately, this narrative ignores the reality of 4 million people kidnapped and enslaved from Africa[15] and the genocide of 54 million Native Americans and indigenous people.[16] These individuals were not immigrants. So when we claim to be a nation of immigrants, we erase their presence and our country's role in their suffering and death.

When (un)learning more about American history, our first step is a counterintuitive one. Before adding knowledge, we must shed knowledge. We have mental models, born of the Declaration of Independence and the Constitution, that are barriers to the learning we want to do. We have narratives, amplified in our textbooks and our holidays, of melting pots and meritocracies. We have assumptions, untested in our experiences and our networks, of what is true. We have unlearning to do.

We Are All Ready

To return to that prairie with the little house, some might question whether my kids were developmentally ready to process the full story. They were. In a study about scientific beliefs, psychologist Deborah Kelemen showed that it is easier to learn correct knowledge at a young age than unlearn incorrect beliefs later, arguing that learning counterintuitive ideas requires similar cognitive resources as becoming a fluent speaker of a second language.[17] Kids especially need practice at unlearning erroneous cause-and-effect relationships.[18]

My kids, like most kids, were ready. I was not. I did not know how to unlearn. I did not know how to reckon. So I did not, dumping that responsibility on my future self and worse, on my children.

In the near-decade since that vacation, it has become harder for me—and for so many of us—to duck responsibility. I feel the pain of our nation, as so many do, and have started to realize that I have contributed to that pain. By not learning and unlearning what needed to be learned and unlearned, I made it harder to see what systems need to change. And I passed this on to my children.

In his book *How the Word Is Passed: A Reckoning with the History of Slavery Across America*, Clint Smith asks, "What would it take—what does it take—for you to confront a false history even if it means shattering the stories you have been told throughout your life? Even if it means having to fundamentally reexamine who you are and who your family has been? Just because something is difficult to accept doesn't mean you should refuse to accept it. Just because someone tells you a story doesn't make that story true."[19]

Humans—especially from individualistic Western cultures—speak of our triumphs, not our failures, and more easily excuse our failings than those of others.[20] Such behavior is so quintessentially human that social scientists call it the fundamental attribution error.[21]

Our "myside bias" leads us to assume the best of ourselves and the worst of those we conquered or who conquered us, while sharing only our side of the story.[22] Our ancestors are aligned with angels.

Parts of history are hard to face. Given our country's founding principles, parts of American history are especially hard to face. As a result, many of us are unaware how individual choices in the past created and upheld systems of oppression that have lasting ramifications today. Most of us still want to turn away.

But for many, the past is not in the past. It lives today, blooming repeatedly in both individual behaviors and the systems that reinforce them. If we do not reckon with the atrocities of the past—including how we have treated African-Americans, Native Americans, Japanese-Americans, and others—we cannot address the disparities and injustices of the present. We cannot understand the rage, resentment, and resignation of so many Americans. We cannot become better Americans or build a better America.

If you follow the news or social media, it seems that we must choose between patriots and wokesters, between loving and bashing our country. I reject this premise. It is no more true than saying a parent must choose between loving and setting boundaries for their child. A parent can do both. In fact, setting boundaries is a form of love, even if the child sometimes melts down and lashes out. If anything, these imperfect moments test and reveal our love. We cannot love only the Instagram versions of our children, or of our country.

If you love this country deeply and believe it can do no wrong, I invite you to consider why. If you have fallen out of love with this country and believe it can do no right, I invite you to consider what brings people here, decade after decade. And if you (like me) are somewhere in between, I invite you to consider how all of your feelings can coexist in the search for a more perfect union.

When we talk about "our" country and "we" the people, we are referring both to real people and abstract systems. We are putting ourselves in the collective pronoun, wrapping ourselves in the metaphorical flag.

But this metaphorical flag has not always wrapped itself around everyone. Many Americans have been and are still excluded from its embrace. The feminist movement, the civil rights movement, the gay rights movement, the disability rights movement, and more . . . each has been a plea and demand to make our collective noun more than a word, to make this country be everyone's country.

Why This Book (and Me, of All People)

I am not a historian. I am not even really a history buff. And this is not a history book. While your golden doodle is better qualified to write a history book than I am, I can offer you psychological tools to cope with the emotional experience of reckoning with past events and making sense of today's news cycle. This book will help you grapple with history, know what to expect, and know what mindset to bring. These topics are not the domain of historians but of psychologists. You need to be prepared for the journey; this book is your travel guide.

My most obvious qualification is my expertise as a social psychologist. Academic research by behavioral scientists can be helpful but difficult to access and understand unless you are a scholar in the field. My training and research allow me to curate these findings with real-world examples to give you an evidence-based and actionable set of tools.

My less obvious—and perhaps more compelling—qualification is my lack of expertise as a historian paired with my love of country. I want to love, not bash, this country. Doing that requires me to learn more and unlearn more of my country's history. Intellectually, this is not difficult. Books, movies, podcasts, and social media accounts are bursting with the information you and I need.

The challenge I feel is psychological and emotional, not intellectual. For me, unlearning whitewashed American history can elicit guilt, shame, and even grief as I lose my idealistic view of my country and its unrealized egalitarian ideals. Grief at mourning the heroic yet hypocritical figures of Jefferson and Washington I grew up admiring. Guilt at sacrificing the truth of Thanksgiving and Columbus Day in favor of the more comforting fable. Shame for what happened in the past and then, shame for my ignorance about it. Guilt, shame, and grief make it hard for me to do the learning and unlearning I need to do.

My first book, *The Person You Mean to Be: How Good People Fight Bias,* was a guidebook for how to be a better person. I wrote the book I felt I needed to read. I made the provocative argument that the more we care about being good people, the harder it is for us to be better people. When we view mistakes as a threat to our good-person identity, we fail to learn from them and thus, we do not grow. If we give up the notion of being a good person and embrace the idea of being a "good-ish" person, those mistakes help us—me—do better.

There is wide, growing, and urgent interest in becoming better people . . . and the psychological challenges of doing so. As social scientists unpack the reality of how the human mind works, it becomes more and more clear that our notions of how to be a good person are naïve. With *A More Just Future,* I will take you on a similar journey through the science that will help us reckon with the past.

As with my first book, I wrote this book because it is the book I know how to write *and* the book I need to read.

Love of Country

I am scared to publish this book. I don't doubt the value of what I am writing or the stakes of the moment. Both are high. But I know that this book will upset a few people and I am a people pleaser, inclined to apologize to anyone who bumps into me on the sidewalk. I don't want a fight or a mic drop. I hate the idea of being labeled as someone who hates America or is ashamed to be an American. Nothing could be further from the truth, and yet, I know that will not be how some people see it. I have stared at the ceiling at 3 a.m. worrying. My anxieties have sowed doubt and slowed me down. I have backspaced perfectly good paragraphs as I have catastrophized the way they will be twisted out of context. In the end, I keep returning to that lovely, confusing Little House on the Prairie and those two kids on my lap.

I know this book is not for everyone. I also know that I am not alone in my struggles to understand the contradictions around me and the confusion within me. Some Americans love this country too much to give up on it. Some Americans used to love this country and need help finding a path out of disillusionment and back to that love. No matter your race, ethnicity, immigrant status, or political affiliation, if you are willing to reckon with the past, this book is for you.

Some, like Michael Harriot, have been trying to tell these stories for ages. Others are hearing—or listening—to them for the first time. Some, like me, are somewhere in the middle. Throughout the book, I have written most directly to those in the earlier stages of reckoning but am hopeful that the tools I offer will also be useful to those looking for vocabulary, arguments, science, stories, and metaphors to bolster the knowledge and work they have been doing for a long time. Whether your reckoning has just begun or is well under way, this book offers a toolkit.

We Have the Tools

A More Just Future is organized in seven chapters, each using stories and science to introduce you to the tools needed to reckon with and unlearn whitewashed history. We begin by tackling the question of how do we start, with the tools of seeing the problem and what I call dressing for the weather. Then we focus on what can we do and how to use the tools of embracing paradox, connecting the dots, and rejecting fables. We close by asking where do we go from here, outlining the tools of taking responsibility and building grit.

With these tools, we can reckon with the past of a nation, this nation, our nation.

Part A

How Do We Start?

– 1 –

See the Problem

You know the greatest lesson of history?
It's that history is whatever the victors say it is. That's the lesson.
Whoever wins, that's who decides the history.
—ANTHONY DOERR

Meghan Lydon's mom was confused. Her daughter was graduating from high school and had a peculiar request. A talented performer with a terrific voice, she had starred in theater productions like *Fiddler on the Roof* and *Hello, Dolly!* She was a funny, outgoing, "pretty mainstream" white student who rarely got lower than an A-minus and played on the tennis team.

Meghan wanted a "not cheap" high school souvenir. "I wanted to keep my Advanced Placement History textbook," Meghan says, laughing. She had finished the course and aced the test. "We weren't able to cover everything from the huge textbook in the course that year," she recalls. "But I really wanted to read the whole thing." With an amused shrug of her shoulders, her mom agreed.

Unsurprisingly, dinner table conversations in Meghan's Rhode Island family often included recaps of what she and her siblings were learning in American history class, Meghan's favorite subject. She had passionate teachers who inspired love of country. The underdog narrative "is so inspiring," she reflects. "It makes you feel patriotic and prideful because you think, That's us, we did it!" This attitude delighted her father, the type of dad who was visibly overcome by awe and reverence when visiting the monuments in Washington, D.C. The anything-is-possible-if-you-work-hard-enough American narrative permeated her history class and her family's belief system. She went to college to major in musical theater with this sense of determination and her high school history textbook, taking nearly enough college history courses to declare a second major.

Meghan is now a twenty-seven-year-old personal trainer (my personal trainer!) and professional actor living in New York City. After an hour of planks and push-ups, we sat in the lounge outside the gym as she shared her story. "I still own that textbook," she says. "But I think about it differently now."

Not a One-Off

A shift began in college. In one course, a professor drew upon current events, including a recent viral video in which white fraternity members on a bus were singing a song about lynching black people. "The national response was that this was a horrible, one-off incident, not us as a nation," Meghan recalls. "I felt that way, too."

Course assignments required students to read primary sources and study what had happened after slavery. "I realized there was no formal taking of responsibility, just generationally sweeping it under the rug," she says. With her classmates, she began to connect the dots from the 1800s to this viral video in present times. "There is a pretty clear cultural and historical line between point A and point B." Reluctantly, she concluded that the "viral video was not a one-off."

She recalled what she learned in high school about slavery, the internment of Japanese-Americans, and the treatment of Native Americans. Slavery was terrible, but a necessary evil for the southern economy. Internment was terrible, but justified by the attack on Pearl Harbor. The treatment of Native Americans was terrible, but more about smallpox than genocide. "The narrative was typically that people didn't know better, or people were scared, or people had no other option," she reflects.

Looking back, she notices a few things. "None of it was in the horrific detail as the reality. I don't remember any first-person accounts," she recalls. "Also, there was an air of 'this doesn't relate to America today.' The emphasis was 'and then we fixed it.' It was very easy to detach yourself from it."

She pauses, and then says, "In contrast, the pride I felt at the good things was not detached at all. It is as if I was deeply moved by the good things but not as fully moved by the bad things. I guess it is hard to reconcile this idea we have of ourselves as the 'best country' with these bad things. That's what people—and I—am grappling with now."

Summer of 2020

In the summer of 2020, as the Black Lives Matter movement gained wider visibility, Meghan read *White Fragility: Why It's So Hard for White People to Talk About Racism*,[1] a book that appeared to suddenly materialize on many white people's nightstands and in book groups. Both influential and controversial, the book prompted thought among many, including Meghan. She recalls thinking, Oh my God, why am I so defensive? Around the same time, she noticed that many of the people she followed on social media were white. "I purposely started seeking out a more diverse group of people to follow," she says. Then Meghan started seeing startling infographics in her social media feeds. She rattles off a few. One offered "your daily dose of unlearning" ("Martin Luther King Jr. was more radical than we remember"); another looked at the origins of the police; yet another examined the segregated history of the American beach.

She pulls out her phone and opens up Instagram. As she scrolls to the post she is describing to me, I ask about the dozens and dozens of posts that she has saved for easy access.

"I used to just use Instagram for scrolling through posts from friends along with fitness content and recipes. Then I realized I could use it to broaden my perspective," she explains. She started following a more diverse group of content creators, in the fitness and recipe spaces relevant to her work, as well as the historical topics that have long fascinated her.

Meghan learned of the Tulsa Massacre of 1921, in which city officials supplied weapons to white mobs who burned down entire black neighborhoods—killing many, leaving thousands homeless, and destroying a vibrant business community known as "Black Wall Street." She learned that her home state of Rhode Island played a central role in slavery, particularly at the ports, with economic exploitation through trade and labor. She learned that her new hometown of New York City had enslaved people in almost every other household,[2] defying the common northern misconception of slavery as a solely southern institution.

Upsetting revelations kept coming. With each one, the history lover in Meghan felt "embarrassed and guilty," but she kept scrolling. Using the research skills she had learned in college, she consulted reliable sources to verify the new information and distinguish it from "alternative facts." To her astonishment, these revelations and more were accurate. "I realized I needed to unlearn and relearn some things," she told me. "And I realized that progress I took for granted like the civil rights movement was far from a given."

Meghan's original sense of inevitable progress exemplifies "hindsight bias." This mental illusion affects everyone and occurs when past events appear predestined, despite much uncertainty at the time.[3] We struggle to imagine an alternate present in which past events had not occurred. One casualty of this quirky mental habit: we underestimate the blood, sweat, and tears that engender social change. With hindsight bias, the present feels inevitable.

While Meghan was flummoxed, she also had an insight. "I realized I could scroll and curate my feed more intentionally. I could save things I really wanted to dig into and come back to them. This could be intellectually stimulating. Honestly, it made Instagram more meaningful to me," she explained. Her new "textbook"—written from multiple per-spectives—had been in her pocket all along.

This realization became more personal while speaking with a group of friends, one of whom was black. Meghan mentioned the American dream and how they were all raised to believe "you could do anything if you worked hard enough." To her surprise, the friend said, "Oh, I wasn't raised that way." Meghan saw the issue immediately. The systemic barri-ers to the American dream were real for her friend and so many others, even today, even if they worked "hard enough." This was not just about understanding the past, but also about understanding the present. And she wanted to do both.

I Love This Country

I asked Meghan if she still loved her country. "Absolutely! I definitely love this country. But my love now is shown more through trying to make it better, just like I do with my training clients." As one of those fitness clients, I am puzzled by the comparison until she reminds me of her pep talks. Taking care of ourselves is an act of love, she exhorts cli-ents. Fixating on perfection or shame leads to the same outcome: doing nothing. When we recognize opportunities to be healthier or stronger, then we move forward. "To me, love is always trying to improve," she says in a firm voice. "To do that, you have to see the problem."

In the rest of this chapter, we follow Meghan's lead to break down what it means to see the problem. We start with how basic psycho-logical principles shape how history is captured, remembered, and documented. Based on the "home team bias," we reflect on how love of country can both help and hurt our country, what I call the "pa-triot's dilemma." We then explore how that bias manifests in many of our textbooks and classrooms, both in the United States and abroad. Finally, we look at how educators are seeing and tackling the problems both as learners and teachers.

Home Team Bias

It was the end of fall in 1952 and as the leaves turned red and yellow, the football season came to a close. This was a tough way to end a season. All-American Dick Kazmaier, Princeton University's halfback, had to leave the game with a mild concussion and a broken nose in the second quarter. Jim Miller, Dartmouth College's quarterback, had to leave the game with a broken leg in the third quarter. Princeton won 13–0. The season was ending in a dramatic fashion.

Accusations of dirty play flew. One Princeton player told the school paper that "Dartmouth was out to get" their star player, while another Princeton player said, "I am completely disgusted . . . with the Dartmouth brand of football."[4] In contrast, the Dartmouth coach proudly stated, "It was one of the best defensive games a Dartmouth team of mine has ever played."[5] The Dartmouth alumni magazine assured its readers that, except for one instance of unsportsmanlike conduct, the charges of dirty play were "manufacture[d]" by Princeton undergraduates writing for the school paper, and then picked up by national media.

To understand those differing accounts, two psychologists recruited students from both schools to participate in a study a week after the game. They began with a survey of students taking introductory and intermediate psychology courses at both schools. Then the researchers asked the students in fraternities and undergraduate clubs to watch a video of the game. Those students also filled out a survey about whether the game "was clean and fairly played, or . . . unnecessarily rough and dirty?," "how many infractions" each team made, and "which team do you feel started the rough play?"

It was as if the Dartmouth and Princeton students had watched two different games. None of the Princeton respondents felt the game was "clean and fair." In fact, they perceived the Dartmouth team as making twice as many infractions as the Dartmouth study participants perceived. Among the Dartmouth participants, 53 percent felt both schools started the foul play; 2 percent felt Princeton started it; (only) 36 percent felt

Dartmouth started it; 9 percent felt it was neither. Among the Princeton students, 11 percent felt both schools started it, while 86 percent felt Dartmouth started it and 3 percent felt it was neither. In other words, only a third of the Dartmouth participants thought it was Dartmouth's fault, while the vast majority of Princeton participants pointed the finger at Dartmouth. The results were the same, regardless of whether a student had attended the game in-person or not.

In some ways, they did. The researchers played the same video for everyone, but the students saw different things in the video. In a paper titled "They Saw a Game," Albert H. Hastorf and Hadley Cantril explained, "A person selects those [occurrences] that have some significance for him from his own egocentric position," which sounds akin to the confirmation bias other researchers would later name, a phenomenon in which people unconsciously see what they want to see.[6] While motivations exist to distort the truth, intentional lies do not fully explain these stark differences in perception. This tendency to pay more attention to what confirms our inklings and less attention to what challenges our inklings also occurs unconsciously. If we were to listen to only one group of students, we would fail to grasp the game in its entirety.

Those Princeton and Dartmouth fans were no different than the rest of us. Imagine you just got home from cheering your favorite team to victory. A friend asks you for a recap. You might describe the heartbreaking error, the funny moment in the stands, the clutch play, the no-good refs. You might remember more of your own team's plays. You might be less forgiving of a lack of sportspersonship from the visiting team than the home team. You might cheer for your team as the good guys and jeer the other team as the bad guys. You might pay extra attention to a couple of the players, whom you once spotted and greeted at a restaurant.

In other words, your home team recap will reflect your natural tendency to know more, notice more, credit more, and forgive more from your own team. This home team bias tendency does not make one evil, just human. When it comes to a football game, our tendency to see the things that confirm our own identity can be simple and straightforward enough. But what about things that are far more fraught, like American history? There the home team might certainly be "American" but it is also all of our other identities we hold, especially those that have been historically meaningful, such as race. Regardless of identity, we do not have to be intentionally biased to be subject to the home team bias.

Once, while Meghan urged me into one more plank and Bruno Mars crooned in the background, I tried to distract her with a summary of the home team bias paper (apparently, Mindy Kaling has good success distracting her trainers, so why not give it a try?!). Meghan responded, "It's like all we know is America's greatest hits."

Greatest Hits

Meghan's statement that we overfocus on the greatest hits resonates with my research. With my colleagues Mahzarin Banaji, Max Bazerman, and Mary Kern, I have written about bounded ethicality,[7] which I sometimes refer to as the psychology of good people.[8] No matter how objective, well trained, and professional we are, we are prone to errors in what we see and perceive, with our minds being pulled toward that which is more consistent with what we already know and more flattering to who we are, whom we love, and whom we identify with. I will never be able to see my children as others see them because our minds are not programmed for objectivity. They are programmed for consistency.

Our minds are also prone to limitations in memory, storage, and processing speed. These constraints lead to bounded rationality, a term first coined by Nobel Prize winner Herb Simon and which led to an expansive field of research in behavioral economics, psychology, and other social sciences.[9] Because of bounded rationality, we may be more likely to remember the apartments we viewed first or last in our search, rather than in the middle. We overattend to vivid statistics, like the probability of dying by terrorist attack, and underattend to drab data, like the probability of dying of cardiovascular disease. Our minds anchor on a particular point of view or value, such as the list price of a car. We are also prone to bounded awareness, a failure to notice, see, and seek out easily available information, because it does not align with our expectations or views.[10] We do not see the conspicuous butter in the fridge when it is in a different place than usual and we somehow miss the error messages on our phones as we scroll through our social media feeds. We need not intend to be unaware, yet we may be deeply unaware.

Bounded awareness, bounded rationality, and bounded ethicality do not apply only to sporting events. The same pattern recurs in marriages, workplaces, pandemics, elections, insurrections, and the recording and learning of history. Our challenge is to see how these natural tendencies are exacerbated by our love of our country, and, as Meghan says, how that makes it harder for us to do better.

The Patriot's Dilemma

I call the phenomenon the "patriot's dilemma": the more we love this country, the less likely we are to do the necessary work to improve it. The more pride we take in our ancestors, the harder it is for us to tell their full stories, both successes and shortcomings. The more we identify with heroes from the past, the more threatened we feel by their subheroic behavior. Paradoxically, the more we love our country's purported ideals, the more difficult it is to see how we fall short of them. Because of the patriot's dilemma, our love for our nation is a barrier to making our nation better.

But this dilemma can be resolved. The key lies in how we think about the past.

We vary in how connected we feel our past is to our present. If my present-day country resembles how I remember my country from the past, I see the past and present as highly connected. Researchers have found that this "historical continuity" can create a sense of stability.[11] This continuity is particularly important for individuals who strongly identify with their country. When the past and the present feel disconnected—perhaps because of societal changes—high-identifying individuals amp up that patriotic identity to provide the stability that the past was not providing. Those who identify less with their country depend less on the continuity between the past and present. In other words, the superpatriotic person (in the very narrow sense of that word) reacts particularly badly when the past and present are out of sync.

The uptick in the conspicuous display of the American flag in recent years, during a time of great social change and upheaval, might be one example of this tendency in action. Of course, whether or not one displays the flag is not the point; the point is the increase in the flag displays for highly identified individuals during a tumultuous time. The before-and-after difference reveals the effect.

In these studies, the researchers also measured the participants' degree of "collective angst," defined as "fear for the future existence of the ingroup."[12] For strong identifiers confronting high historical discontinuity, collective angst and opposition to immigration were high. So, in addition to the flag displaying, these individuals are in ears-straight-up and teeth-bared mode, fearful of change and aggressive to outsiders.

To recap these research findings, psychologists have robust evidence that we are all prone to the home team bias, in which we see things through our own eyes and those of the groups we identify with. This tendency means that we are likely to have a different perspective than others, but remain convinced that our perspective is correct. When times are unstable and we feel that our group is threatened, we go on the defensive. This tendency is particularly true for those highly identified with their groups, leaving us with the patriot's dilemma in which we are so invested in our home team narrative, we are unable to see another perspective.

The patriot's dilemma is worsened when the patriot is a member of a dominant group. Political scientist Diana Mutz challenged the prevalent "economic anxiety" theory of Donald Trump's rise by tracking political attitudes of people from dominant groups (whites, Christians, men).[13] Her research demonstrates that the growing numbers and status of nonwhite groups—as well as globalization—contributes to a defensive reaction among members of dominant groups that is not explained by economic anxiety. Rather, she finds those who perceive threats seek to reestablish status hierarchies. She calls this phenomenon dominant group status threat. This is more than home team bias; it is home team defensiveness.

Critical Race Theory Has Everything and Nothing to Do with This

In the late 1970s, Norman Lear changed television with shows like *All in the Family* and *The Jeffersons*. These hit shows brought real-life tensions in American families to the center of the fictional shows those same families were watching. Rocky race relations and bigoted backlash were discussed openly in politically divided white families like the Bunkers and economically striving black families like the Jeffersons. While more than a decade had passed since the Civil Rights Act of 1964 and Dr. Martin Luther King Jr.'s aspirational challenge that society not judge his children by the color of their skin, these shows rejected the color-blind narrative. Viewers could relate: racial disparity was a pervasive and persistent presence in their daily lives.

But why? In the context of this clearly racialized reality, legal scholars like Derrick Bell, Kimberlé Crenshaw, and Richard Delgado challenged the narrative that race—and racism—no longer explained racial disparities. From their and others' work, critical race theory (CRT) was born.[14] Their goal was to develop an intellectual framework to study if and how racism is embedded in systems, policies, and laws. Like most academic fields, CRT is a narrow, deep area of work to allow for rigor and precision in the research. For the next forty years, the topic was studied by academics and largely unknown by nonacademics.

Fast-forward to 2021. The teaching of history became front-page news, as did jargon previously reserved for that small circle of legal scholars.[15]

Critical race theory went from being an area of legal scholarship with a precise academic focus to a household word with little agreed-upon meaning. Unfortunately, most people using the acronym *CRT*—which can stand for both critical race theory as well as culturally responsive teaching—have little understanding of either. CRT became a bucket term for describing anything ranging from mentioning racism to teaching about slavery to sharing historical facts to the original legal analysis framework.

In education, some are using CRT to describe anything that relates to mentioning nonwhite people in schools, whether it be a young-adult novel written by a nonwhite author or a history lesson about how nonwhite people were treated or an opportunity to examine one's implicit biases about nonwhite people. None of these are actual examples of critical race theory.

It is as if pomegranate—a specific fruit—suddenly became synonymous with food, such that every item on a restaurant's menu was now simply labeled pomegranate. Pasta, pancakes, pumpkins, and pizza—we just call them all "pomegranate." As a result, the menu is confusing and the ordering process counterproductive. The original meaning of pomegranate is lost. We are using the same words but it is unclear if we are talking about the same thing.

The Present Reflects the Past

Put simply, critical race theory "is a way to talk openly about how America's history has had an effect on our society and institutions today."[16] The theory takes the stance that existing laws, structures, and institutions are not as race-neutral as they appear. They are a product of the society in which they were created and thus may reflect that society's racism, past and present. Historical patterns of racism remain in our legal system, and legacies of those patterns remain in society.

For example, the CROWN Act is legislation that prohibits discrimination based on hairstyles and hair textures in workplaces and schools.[17]

Several states and cities have passed the law, but it has yet to receive the necessary U.S. Senate votes to become federal law. Without this law, nothing stops an employer from essentially requiring a black employee to use toxic chemicals to straighten their hair in order to meet "professionalism" or "dress code" requirements, rather than wearing an afro, braids, cornrows, or another natural style. A critical race theory perspective would cite the lack of legal protection for non-European hairstyles and textures as evidence that whiteness is built into our country's legal structures and institutions.

Within the legal scholarship world, sizable evidence supports this theory. For example, critical race scholars have shown that the punishment for drug offenses varies widely by the type of drug being used. There is no difference in the public health or personal risk consequences between crack cocaine and powder cocaine. However, there is a notable difference in the demographics of who tends to use these drugs: the majority of crack cocaine offenders are black; the majority of powder cocaine offenders are white. Beginning in the 1980s and 1990s with "war on drugs" and "tough on crime" campaigns, sentences for possession of one gram of crack cocaine were 100 times longer than those for one gram of powder cocaine.[18] The Fair Sentencing Act in 2010 changed the ratio from 100:1 to 18:1, still a stark gap.[19]

This superficially nondiscriminatory set of laws leads to a racially discriminatory outcome. This is the premise of critical race theory: apparently color-blind laws can still have non-color-blind outcomes and historical roots.

We Can Handle the Emotions

Understanding critical race theory requires knowledge of how the concept of race has evolved in our country and the historical roots of laws. While critical race theory is not about knowing history for history's sake, it does require some historical digging to contextualize what would otherwise appear to be an odd (at best) or hateful (at worst) outcome. As the field of critical race theory has evolved over the past few decades, the approach has proven useful in fields outside of law, including education, political science, and American studies. The idea remains the same. What appears race-neutral in the present may actually be discriminatory when its origins and current-day impacts are revealed.

Whether we use the actual definition of CRT, or the pomegranate distortions of the term, a similar concern arises. Some worry that this pedagogical approach leaves students feeling undeserved shame and guilt, and therefore should not be in our schools. In many states, laws are being proposed or passed prohibiting teaching CRT in K–12 schools, which is confusing, given the unlikely possibility that any K–12 school was teaching graduate-level legal scholarship.

I understand the worry, but I think we are approaching the issue the wrong way. Yes, reckoning with our country's past might lead to guilt and shame. In fact, that is exactly why I decided to write this book. While I am not a legal expert on critical race theory, I know it is a misconception that the CRT's goal is to teach American history in a way that vilifies and shames anyone. Those emotions may arise, not as the goal but as a by-product. And we can handle them.

The idea that facing our whitewashed past will evoke uncomfortable emotions is far from new and has little to do with critical race theory. That is an issue more for psychologists like me than for legal scholars.* My stance is that we teach CRT (or as it should be called, history) and prepare ourselves to grapple with all the feelings that it brings.

The very fact that different accounts of historical events can evoke different emotions for different people reveals where part of the problem lies. Not only are we prone to the home team bias in our minds, we are also prone in our history books, our schools, and our classrooms. Seeing history for what it is, and what it is not, is part of seeing the problem.

---

*In fact, I contracted to write this book in 2019, two years before the school board and national news debates over critical race theory took off in spring 2021. These issues are not new.

See History for What It Is

If history is prone to some of the same biases as a recap from a home team fan, where does that leave us? Our first challenge is to notice how we rarely learn about or teach history with this limitation in mind. A prominent source of our historical knowledge is formal education, from a nursery school story about George Washington not telling a lie to a high school textbook delineating key battles of the Civil War. Teachers and textbooks carry an air of authority, and students like me and even Meghan often receive classroom history as a series of immutable facts.

To see history for what it is, we must first and foremost recognize that it is a story. And stories have a perspective. Educator Duncan Koerber wanted to create this awareness with a personal history assignment.[20] He asked his students to write a classroom history, a family history, a local history, a personal history, or a piece of creative historical fiction, and then to reflect on the experience of being a historian.

If I did his assignment, I might write about my parents' experiences as refugees during the 1947 Partition of India and Pakistan. First, I would need to figure out what was true. I would need to reconcile the multiple family members' perspectives about what happened and when. They might have individual perspectives on whether "refugee" was the right descriptor. When there were factual contradictions about what belongings they took or where they stayed at night, I would have to decide how to deal with the discrepancy. My mother's family and my father's family had very different experiences in 1947; no doubt every family had a unique experience. I would need to somehow account for this variation in stating what was true.

Both of my parents were raised in mostly Hindu families, so I would be sharing their perspective, not those of entirely Muslim families or of Sikh families. Conflicts and violence were pervasive, and so was (is) finger-pointing for the causes of the conflicts and violence.

Thus, determining the truth would not be straightforward. As one of Koerber's students reflected, "Yes, I feel that my stories represent the truth of what happened, from my perspective. I mean, in a way, I feel like there is no such thing as 'truth' because everyone sees things in a different way." I would have to sort through everyone's "truths" in order to figure out what was true.

Second, I would depend on memory and documentation. My parents were children at the time. Trauma would make remembering difficult as well. For my father, who saw thousands of dead bodies during the journey as a young boy, painful memories are difficult to revisit. Surely that trauma would affect his memory. Similarly, some of Koerber's students struggled: "I had a hard time remembering details, especially the one about childhood because it was so long ago."

Third, I would need to decide what to include and exclude. It is neither desirable nor feasible for historians to include everything. Do I treat Great Britain as the nostalgic hero or traumatizing villain in dividing my parents' homeland, or not mention Great Britain at all? Do I explore Mohandas Gandhi's role? Once I include something, does that make it more likely others will as well? Or, once I exclude something, is it forgotten forever? And (how) do I tell stories that will potentially upset family members who have already endured so much hardship?

My micro-experience of being a historian highlights how little of history is pure fact. When I move from being a passive recipient of history produced by others to a producer of historical accounts, the experience strips me of the illusion of history as a series of immutable facts. Historians Richard Marius and Mel Page explain: "Historians must always put something of themselves into the stories they tell; never are they empty vessels through which the records of the past spew forth as if they were an untouched truth about the past."[21]

Try your own "doing history" thought experiment in your mind or on paper. What do you include and exclude? Which perspectives do you represent? What is not well remembered or documented? Now think about how the challenges you experienced would grow exponentially if the assignment were to capture the history of an event affecting not just you or your family, but an entire society.

No matter how thoughtful or thorough the producer of the historical account, the history will always be told through their lens, the product of their mind. And everything we receive is the product of how our own mind works, including the good-guys-win mindset and the home team bias. When we know this, we can step outside the history we are consuming and be "meta" about it, just as historiographers must do.

Be a Historiographer

Historiographers are in constant conversation with themselves. They are historians who study how we study history. They examine whose perspectives are represented and whose are not, what has been forgotten or undocumented, what narratives do not align with primary sources, and what primary sources have been lost or destroyed. In the "doing history" assignment above, students experience the work of the historian when they write history and the work of the historiographer when they reflect about the process of writing history.

Historiographer James Loewen gave himself an unenviable, multiyear homework assignment. He sat in a room at the Smithsonian Institution with a pile of twelve of the most popular American history textbooks from the mid-1990s. They averaged 4.5 pounds and 888 pages . . . each. He read every single page. In 2006 he updated his analysis by reading six new books; each text averaged almost six pounds and 1,150 pages.

Loewen shares his findings from analyzing eighteen textbooks in the updated, 2006 edition of *Lies My Teacher Told Me.*[22] For example, only nine of the eighteen textbooks listed the word *racism* (or a similar term like "racial discrimination" in the index). Even in those nine that listed the term, only one actually defined it in the text; several of the nine listed the term but did not address the issue. Rather, the term signaled coverage of a topic like slavery or segregation, which was somehow explained without mention of racism.

This omission means that if a student were to look up racism in the index, they might be referred to pages discussing segregation. But the explanation of segregation would not mention racism. This perplexes me. It would be like looking up smoking in the index and being referred to a section on lung cancer that never mentioned smoking. Perhaps more damningly, if a reader were to *not* consult the index (as few readers do), they would read an entire explanation of segregation or slavery with no mention of racism.

Loewen notes an improvement over time in the truth-telling about the brutality of slavery in many of the texts, but a startling silence on the people committing the brutal acts. "They present slavery virtually as uncaused, a tragedy, rather than a wrong perpetrated by some people on others." All of the textbooks failed to wrestle with or deeply cover the paradox of founding fathers who enslaved Africans. As a result, these texts form an influential system that whitewashes rather than reckons with our past.

In a more recent 2017 study, the Southern Poverty Law Center endeavored to understand teaching and learning about slavery in American schools.[23] They assembled a panel of experts—the SPLC staff, a history professor whose research focuses on slavery, and an independent education researcher. They developed a thirty-point rubric to evaluate how the texts depicted slavery. The panel reviewed ten highly used history texts and surveyed 1,700 social studies teachers and 1,000 high school seniors.

The average grade: 46 percent. Hasan Kwame Jeffries, the professor on the panel, told the *New York Times,* "We are committing educational malpractice."[24] Items on the rubric included how the history of slavery was integrated throughout the book—the connecting of the dots between the causes and effects. The poor grade reflects how disconnected slavery is from how the rest of our country's history is told.

This poor grade is not an esoteric statistic or academic exercise. Meghan, the star history student, was unfamiliar with these studies when I mentioned them. Yet she bears the burden of this low grade. Because she learned about slavery in a detached and disconnected way as a child, she was not as well equipped as she wanted to be to understand today's world and how it came to be. As an adult, she is now having to unlearn and relearn the topic. As someone who loves her country and takes pride in knowing its history, this patriot's dilemma is doubly painful, as she has to face a reality she did not know about and the reality of her ignorance. She read, bought, and still owns the high school textbook, so why did she not know? If someone as passionate about history as her did not know, what chance do people like me have?

Perhaps Norman Lear had it right. We need to show things for how they are. Perhaps critical race theory has it right. We need to show where things came from. Perhaps Meghan has it right. We need to revisit the textbook.

Mommy, Where Do Textbooks Come From?

I do not envy history teachers. They must cover a staggering amount of material. Young people are notoriously myopic, so it is difficult to make the subject relevant. State standards limit teachers' capacity to innovate. And the history textbook itself is the product of highly politicized negotiation. One education reporter writes that "its very construction is essentially a compromise between experts and politicians, groups with sometimes competing agendas . . . they pass through innumerable hands before they ever reach a classroom."[25] Those hands include the people who write the state social studies standards; politicians who write state laws; and panels of appointees who review drafts and then submit their edits to publishers. In other words, non-historians and non-educators play a significant role in how history teachers teach, which would be something like non-athletes and non-coaches playing a significant role in how a sports team plays. Historical expertise does not solely determine what is taught in our classrooms.

Understanding this process helps us understand textbooks as subjective accounts. An investigation by the *New York Times* compared textbooks from California and Texas side by side. Same publisher, same title, same authors. They found significant variation between what was taught. For example, a student in California will learn about redlining and housing discrimination after World War II; a student in Texas will not. This difference has meaningful impact. Without this knowledge, the blatant differences in where black and white people live in the United States and the resources of those communities will appear to be arbitrary or a product of individual choices, not the product of past and present systems.

Let's put this in context. I graduated from high school in 1986. Like Meghan, I had terrific teachers, but unlike Meghan, I had no particular fondness for history or my textbook. Most likely I learned from one or more of the texts Loewen analyzed in my history courses, as did anyone who graduated from high school in the United States before 2006.

When I review the very short subset of Loewen's findings above, I notice what we did not learn. We did not learn how to talk about racism. We did not learn to see the problem. We did not learn how to emotionally prepare for feelings of shame, guilt, or denial . . . what I think of as dressing for the weather. We did not learn how to embrace the paradox of a history filled with both beauty and brutality or to connect the dots between what happened before and what is happening now. We did not learn how to recognize and reject fables that seem better suited for children than adults. And we did not learn how to take responsibility for harm or to build the grit needed to stick with the work of building a more perfect union. There are essential tools for this work that we were never given.

Now we are taking a pop quiz on material we never covered. No wonder we struggle to grasp systemic racism, unconscious bias, and white supremacy. No wonder our country is struggling to move forward from the past. No wonder we are immersed in a confused and emotional debate over critical race theory.

The point of learning about the past is to serve us in the present. How and what we remember is not intended to shame us, but to protect us from our own home team bias. If we fail to remember what happened then, we fail to see what is happening now.

Let's Look at Apartheid

In the Afrikaans language, *apartheid* means "apartness." Beginning in 1948, the National Party, which controlled the South African government at the time, began implementing a series of programs and laws that divided the country by race. Where you lived and worked depended on whether you were classified as Bantu (all black Africans), Coloured (mixed race), white, or Asian (Indian and Pakistani).

This racial classification also determined whether you could move around freely without documents, what jobs you could apply for, whether you could own land, what public facilities you could use, whom you could date or marry, and what schools your children could attend. While whites comprised 20 percent of the population, 80 percent of the country's land was allocated for their use only.[26] Only whites could vote and hold political office. Protesters were regularly killed or arrested. Millions of people were forcibly removed from their homes. Migrant laborers were exploited and beaten while doing dangerous work. Families were separated.

None of this is ancient history. Talk show host Trevor Noah, not even forty years old, was a child under apartheid and puts it bluntly in his memoir, *Born a Crime: Stories from a South African Childhood:* "In America you had the forced removal of the native onto reservations coupled with slavery followed by segregation. Imagine all three of those things happening to the same group of people at the same time. That was apartheid."[27]

Nelson Mandela and other activists spent decades trying to abolish apartheid, which Mandela chronicles in his memoir, *Long Walk to Freedom*.[28] Mandela was imprisoned for his activism for twenty-seven years and continued to push for change from prison. Finally, in the early 1990s, the legal infrastructure of apartheid began to be dismantled and by the mid-1990s, Mandela became the country's president. While many de facto forms of apartheid remained, its legal foundation had been toppled.

Knowledge in the Blood

In the aftermath of apartheid, a black scholar named Jonathan Jansen became the first black rector and vice chancellor of the University of the Free State in South Africa and the first black dean of education at the historically white University of Pretoria. He was tasked with leading white South African students into a new chapter of their country's future, a generation living through one of the most "dramatic social transitions of the twentieth century."

The University of Pretoria was a central force in apartheid. The school served as a feeder of white civil servants who would serve the apartheid government. "Scholars" used their respective disciplines to claim scientific legitimacy for apartheid. Many of the nation's most influential leaders, businesspeople, judges, researchers, and athletes were university alumni. Under apartheid, Jansen explains, "There was no racial tension, because white instructors taught white students about white society with a white curriculum."[29]

As he was entering what he called the "heart of whiteness," several questions dogged Jansen. He wanted to learn how white students remembered apartheid, how young Afrikaners who never lived under apartheid perceived that time, and how whites born at the same time Mandela exited prison understood their country. In his book *Knowledge in the Blood: Confronting Race and the Apartheid Past,* Jansen considers those questions alongside his lived experience. He explains the title of his book:

> Knowledge in the blood for me means knowledge embedded in the emotional, psychic, spiritual, social, economic, political, and psychological lives of a community. Such is the knowledge transmitted faithfully to the second generation of Afrikaner students. It is not, therefore, knowledge that simply dissipates like the morning mist under the pressing sunshine of a new regime of truth; if it were, then curriculum change would be a relatively straightforward matter.

Knowledge in the blood is habitual, a knowledge that has long been routinized in how the second generation see the world and themselves, and how they understand others. It is emphatic knowledge that does not tolerate ambiguity; this dead certainty was long given its authority by a political and theological order that authorized such knowledge as singular, sanctified, and sure. But it is also a defensive knowledge that reacts against and resists rival knowledge, for this inherited truth was conceived and delivered in the face of enemies.[30]

What Happened

As Jansen observed how his white students, their parents, and his colleagues thought about apartheid, he extrapolated three prevailing narratives: 1) nothing happened, 2) something happened, now get over it, and 3) terrible things happened.

In the "nothing happened" narrative, apartheid was a necessary and useful way of creating social order and bolstering black people's capacity to function as equals. When the time was right, it was always planned that apartheid would end and blacks would be given things like the right to vote. In this narrative, no violence, oppression, or dispossession occurred. Everyone benefited from apartheid. In the "nothing happened" narrative, nothing bad happened.

The "something happened" narrative acknowledges rogue individuals—bad apples. But there was a broader need for apartheid and whatever harm was done is over, so now "get over it." A popular South African song captured this narrative. Translated into English, its title is "no longer," with lyrics about refusing to apologize anymore.[31]

Finally, there is the "terrible things happened" narrative. This group came to the narrative in different ways. Some opposed apartheid all along. Others gradually came to understand its wrongs, mostly around and after 1994. Still others had a dramatic and singular epiphany. This narrative leads to real reckoning.

Jansen watched white Afrikaner students whose upbringing offered a particular racist narrative adjust to living and learning with black students. Those who felt that nothing happened or something happened (now get over it) struggled the most. When the truth or a "counternarrative" was revealed, he noted their reaction tended to be "aggressive and angry, as the single story of an innocent past starts to unravel in front of their eyes."

Narrative Systems in the United States

While Jansen's observations are particular to the cultural and historical context of South Africa, the similarities to the United States are striking. In the United States, the nothing-happened group sees our country's treatment of blacks, Native Americans, and others as means to an end, the price to pay for progress, security, and prosperity. If anything, according to this narrative, those groups benefited from how they were treated. Similarly, to some in South Africa, apartheid "overall was a brilliant scheme for keeping racial order and peace." The white architects of apartheid are to be lauded for understanding the needs of blacks.

As in South Africa, the something-happened group sees our country's wrongs as deep, historical issues, so long ago. Once slavery ended, our country manifested its destiny and it is time to get over the distant past. Meghan's recollection of how she learned American history aligns with this narrative. If anything, today's society favors those harmed in the past, goes this narrative.

Finally, the terrible-things-happened narrative connects the past to the present. It can be found among those who have been heartbroken for decades and those for whom George Floyd's murder was a turning point. Real reckoning and the progress it seeds require this narrative.

Trevor Noah's recollection also aligns with the "something happened" narrative. He writes, "In South Africa, the atrocities of apartheid have never been taught that way. We weren't taught judgment or shame. We were taught history the way it's taught in America. In America, the history of racism is taught like this: 'There was slavery and then there was Jim Crow and then there was Martin Luther King Jr. and now it's done. It was the same for us.' Apartheid was bad. Nelson Mandela was freed. 'Let's move on.'"

As Jansen explores how these narratives are perpetuated over generations, he focuses on curriculum, recalling an oft-told story with the punch line, "Show me your curriculum and I'll tell you who is in power." Easiest to see, children learn the official curriculum from textbooks. Less visible is the hidden, or unofficial curriculum. Finally, and least obvious, students learn the null curriculum, what is not included. We see the parallel to what students like Meghan do—and do not—learn in history classes. The narratives act as powerful systems.

A German Thought Experiment

Susan Neiman spent her childhood in the American South and much of her adulthood in Germany. In her book *Learning from the Germans: Race and the Memory of Evil,* she compares how Germans have engaged with the Holocaust and Nazi history to how Americans have engaged with the history of slavery and racism.[32] The contrast, she reports, is striking. In Germany, students learn from a very early age that "terrible things happened."

References to Nazi atrocities and the Holocaust abound in German artwork, literature, television, and movies. A football-field-sized memorial sits in the center of Berlin. "Stumbling stone" markers sit in front of the homes where Jewish residents once lived before being arrested by Nazi authorities. The public reminders to reckon are pervasive. While unrepentant Germans certainly exist and Germany could do plenty more, the country's collective memory includes vivid, salient reminders of past horrors and the collective knowledge includes the indisputable, unfathomable fact of millions of people murdered and many more held in concentration camps.

Neiman encourages a thought experiment, wondering what similar reminders might be in the United States. A slavery memorial in the center of Washington, D.C.? Markers on every building in the country built by enslaved people? Slavery museums in every state where people were enslaved? My guess is yes, yes, and yes.

Clearly, the United States and Germany differ. What surprised Neiman most was the recency of this difference. When she reviewed postwar German writing—such as memoirs and novels—she found little evidence of reckoning. Rather, she found great denial, little remorse, and even a posture of victimhood over lost property and lives. She compared the "moral myopia" of the time to the Lost Cause mentality following the Civil War in which the realities of the Confederate support for slavery were mythologized.

Neiman argues that things changed in the 1960s, when the children and grandchildren of Nazis watched the televised Eichmann and Auschwitz trials. Appalled, they became active (un)learners and began to reckon with their dark past. The rise of the alt-right in Germany and elsewhere makes clear that it has not been a complete success, but the contrast with the United States is clear. Reckoning is taking longer in the United States but perhaps we can learn from Germany. Perhaps we are in a twenty-first-century awakening, propelled by social media and television, and trickling down into our schools.

Let's Get Back to the Fundamentals

When I caught Jared Urban on the phone, he was in Zionsville, Indiana, an Indianapolis suburb with a leafy, brick-lined main street and an ice cream shop loved by kids from neighboring towns. A white high school history teacher and football coach, he was heading to a COVID-era football practice as in-person practices resumed with social distancing. "We are doing lots of conditioning and technique stuff," he told me. While the circumstances were not ideal, he noticed that his players, and his history students, were focusing on the fundamentals. "There is some knowledge gained through this that we would not have ordinarily gained."

When teaching history, Jared has long favored the fundamentals—primary sources and first-person perspectives. He often remembers a story told by one of his college professors. The professor was Hispanic and when growing up in Colorado would sometimes be taunted by kids saying that he and his family should "go home." Ironically, his family had been there for generations longer than the bullies.

"Well, this is home," he would retort. "My family has lived here for hundreds and hundreds of years, way before this was even the United States." The declaration to "go home" was ironic, at best, and reflected their narrow perspective of American history.

His professor's story, Jared says, speaks to the importance of multiple first-person perspectives, in which the people within an experience or culture report their own story. If the story were a football game like the one played in 1952 between Dartmouth and Princeton, it would include the perspectives of players from both teams, fans, coaches, and family members, not only the perspective of one single player. Voices, like those of his professor's family, "have been deliberately erased," says Jared, yet "those voices and their narrative matter more than anyone else's."

So Jared was intrigued when his colleague Kris Devereaux offered him and his colleagues an opportunity. Kris served as the assistant superintendent of academics in the district. Her vision was to take several dozen educators on a professional development trip in February 2020 to visit the U.S. Holocaust Memorial Museum, the National Museum of the American Indian, and the National Museum of African American History and Culture in Washington, D.C., as well as the Legacy Museum and the National Memorial for Peace and Justice in Montgomery, Alabama.

While that itinerary was common, the focus was unique. With a force-of-nature spirit, Kris had a vision. Like Jared, Kris saw the risk of stories told from a single perspective in the classroom and wanted to dive deep into multiple perspectives and multiple narratives. She wanted to invite each educator to first examine their own identities and how those identities might make them more or less aware of certain perspectives. Then she wanted to create an experience where each educator could access a range of perspectives about American history. Threaded throughout, she wanted her participants to view this as not just an intellectual exercise, but also as an emotional one. To sustain their efforts, they would need to cope with the guilt, shame, and grief that arose. Her ambitious vision was that social studies teachers would return home inspired to revise their instructional practices, curricula, and materials.

Kris began recruiting teachers. One of them was Shawn Wooden, a veteran black teacher, administrator, and principal. A few months after the trip, I asked Shawn about his decision to sign up. Kris's vision drew him in. "I already know the history of Montgomery. I am not meaning to be cold, but if you look at it in a tourist kind of way, you might feel, 'Okay, I did that, what will I do next?'" he told me.

"That's not why we did it. We did it to make our community better for those who have been discriminated against and inform the teaching in our very wealthy suburban community." Shawn added, with a smile in his voice, "I love that every single person I talk to about this asked if it was my idea and that it wasn't. Kris [who is white] had the courage to go to her superiors and school board to propose this and ask for funding."

Exhausting and Exhilarating

Once the recruiting was complete, Kris invited the group into pre-work discussions and readings, preparing them for both the intellectual and emotional work ahead. She knew that hearing narratives that conflicted with their own would be demanding, both intellectually and emotionally.* She expected they would be both exhausted and

---

*I met Kris when she read my first book and reached out to ask me for my help in designing the trip, unaware that I was working on this highly relevant second book. While I rarely accept paid consulting assignments, the opportunity to offer guidance on tools (such as those in this book) and learn from the participants' experiences was too fascinating to decline.

exhilarated. Even those who had a solid knowledge base would be exposed to a range of specific perspectives as well as a more experiential and emotional form of learning.

As Kris predicted, the trip was challenging. "Some people struggled with questions of faith. They wondered how this [injustice] could happen alongside their beliefs of a just God," she remembered. "I could just see it on their faces, that they were struggling," she recalls. Good guys were supposed to win. Baked into the emotional struggle was the shame of confronting their own ignorance: some of the narratives they were hearing were new to them, a group of well-trained, well-educated, well-intended social studies teachers.

Stevie Frank, a white writing and social studies teacher in Zionsville, was one of those teachers. Stevie had thought critically about history before. In fact, she cowrote an article[33] in 2014 that began, "Many of us grew up trusting the information that our textbooks provided." The article shares her own journey to realizing the importance of multiple perspectives and exercises she had used with her own students. One exercise takes students into the perspective of an indigenous boy who questions the motives of a captain and his crew arriving on his shores. The students later realize the captain was Christopher Columbus. In another coauthored article,[34] she offered a framework for how to help students think critically about history.

Still, Stevie says, the experience "changed me." While she describes herself as someone who does not cry often in front of others, she found herself crying in a bathroom stall multiple times. She kept asking herself, "Why didn't I know more about this? Why was I not painted a picture of how bad this truly was?"

Perhaps the difference was the visceral experience of hearing first-hand accounts on the trip. I asked her how she would incorporate this in her classroom. "I came back ready to do this," she said. She wanted her students to have the same rich learning experience she had just had.

Less than a month after the trip ended, the COVID-19 pandemic erupted in the United States. Nonetheless, Stevie remained determined. "I spent hours combing through the Smithsonian websites for primary sources and we used them online," she explains. She offered students an array of firsthand accounts (for example, related to the Underground Railroad) to experience. Each student then selected a primary source from the selection and did a video reflection about what they learned and what feelings it brought up for them.

Tell the Stories

I asked Shawn how the trip would affect his work as a teacher-turned-administrator. "I think I will share more of my own family's oral history," he says. It was something he had done occasionally, and he wanted to do it more often. Shawn's grandfather passed away when Shawn was young, but his grandmother often shared his stories. While his grandfather fought for his country in World War II, his grandparents were apart for the first three years of their marriage. When he finally returned via ship from England, there was a warm homecoming welcome. "It was huge," Shawn tells me.

Then the soldiers boarded buses to return to Indianapolis. The hero's welcome became a Jim Crow rebuff . . . for the black soldiers, that is. Shawn's grandfather had to stay on the bus while his white buddies bought him food to eat outside. "To give that sacrifice and then to come home and not be able to walk in a restaurant even in uniform," Shawn says, pausing for a moment. "I think we can paint a better picture. I'm going to help teachers tell this story. The oral history matters. I think we can help this connect for the kids."

Jared said, "One of the best things about our trip was getting the idea across that what we teach is an incomplete history. There are narratives that are not included that have to be included to paint a full narrative of what the United States really is. If you really wanna value a country, you have to look at its good, its bad, and its ugly at the same weight. And if we don't do that, we don't do ourselves a service of really becoming how great we could really become."

Students like Meghan want to learn and educators like Kris, Stevie, Shawn, and Jared want to teach. Many of us, like them, love our country and want to make it better. Our first tool is to see the problem—in how our minds work, how our textbooks are written, and how our patriotism bounds us. By seeing the psychological and institutional systems that make up the problem, we can address them and mitigate their impact. But how? We tackle that next.

Dress for the Weather

There's no such thing as bad weather,
only unsuitable clothing.
—ALFRED WAINWRIGHT

Sunscreen can be the difference between lovely memories of the beach and painful burns. Hat and gloves separate an exhilarating walk in a winter wonderland from an agonizing frostbite march. An umbrella in hand ensures you look crisp at your first meeting of the day, while an umbrella forgotten sends you to the restroom to salvage your look while the meeting starts without you. Dressing for the weather can make all the difference. In this chapter, we look at the stormy emotions that can arise when we are reckoning with the past and how to dress for that kind of weather.

Finding Your Roots

The television industry has stoked our love for nostalgia and personal history with reality shows like *Genealogy Roadshow, Who Do You Think You Are?*, and especially *Finding Your Roots*, which is hosted by Harvard historian Henry Louis "Skip" Gates Jr. and promises to "get into the

DNA of American culture."[1] *Finding Your Roots* is one of PBS's most popular shows, largely because of spellbinding moments where celebrities react to surprising reveals about their family's past.

In each episode of *Finding Your Roots,* guests receive a "book of life" that traces their ancestry. The show's researchers plumb genetic code, archival records, and other historical artifacts to uncover unexpected family connections and secrets. Sometimes the guest learns about a long-lost relative "hidden for generations within the branches of their family trees."[2] Each episode weaves together several guests and their story lines, revealing similarities and differences in their lineages.

It is great television. Superstar couple Kyra Sedgwick and Kevin Bacon are gobsmacked to discover that they are ninth cousins, once removed.[3] Tina Fey learns that her family came to the United States on the suggestion of her ancestor's buddy, Benjamin Franklin.[4] Sarah Jessica Parker hears that her ancestor was branded a witch in the Salem Witch Trials.[5] Congressman John Lewis breaks down in tears upon seeing his great-great-great grandfather's voter registration paperwork from 1867, a brief window between slavery and Jim Crow when formerly enslaved people were allowed to vote, nearly a century before the "Bloody Sunday" on which Lewis was beaten by police as he fought for voting rights.[6]

The set, tone, and vibe of the show depart from dry historical terrain; it is emotional. The guests seem to expect the unexpected, and the reveals allow viewers to witness unscripted emotional responses. I wonder how a celebrity prepares for the taping. It is unlike a movie set, where they come with lines memorized, and unlike a red-carpet event, where they come glammed out, prepared to pose.

On this show, coming prepared is like dressing for the weather . . . emotionally. When we watch a sad movie or attend a funeral, we put ourselves in the right frame of mind and steady ourselves, like bringing an emotional umbrella. And just like some people are always cold or always hot, some people are going to be especially prone to this stormy weather . . . the patriot's dilemma says that the more we love this country, the less prepared we are going to be to deal with its realities.

I am going to tell you about a celebrity who was well prepared for this . . . and one who was not. But first some background on the stormy weather.

Far from Ahistorical

The popularity of *Finding Your Roots* refutes George Santayana's famous worry: "Those who cannot remember the past are condemned to repeat it"[7] and the stereotype that Americans are futuristic, ahistorical time travelers without a rewind button. Data suggests that Americans love the past. According to one study, in the previous twelve months, 91 percent of Americans had looked at photos of the past, 81 percent had watched TV shows or movies about the past, 64 percent had attended a family reunion or some other reunion, 57 percent had visited a history museum or historic site, 40 percent had participated in a hobby related to the past, 36 percent had worked on a family tree/history, 29 percent had written in a journal, and 20 percent had taken part in a group devoted to studying/preserving or presenting the past.[8] When it comes to mental time travel, we like to rewind.

In addition, consumer DNA testing has boomed, with approximately 1 in 25 American adults taking a test in 2017.[9] Family genealogy is a rapidly expanding hobby, fueled by the internet and the availability of digital records. In 2014, *Time* magazine published an article titled "How Genealogy Became Almost as Popular as Porn."[10] According to the article, genealogy is the second most popular hobby in the United States (behind gardening) and the second most visited category of websites (behind porn).[11]

Americans are far from ahistorical. In fact, we are becoming *more* historically minded. Still, we don't want just any history. We want personal history. We love looking back at *our* past, *our* stories, and *our* ancestors. *Finding Your Roots* taps into core desires around our collective identity, love of nostalgia, and desire to bask in reflected glory. Science explains each of these desires.

Social Identities

I carry many identities. My individual identities—such as dog mom—distinguish me from others. These are identities that I care about and when someone questions them, I feel threatened. Recently I was walking our puppy and his foot got caught in a door. It was terrifying, but after a cuddle, he was fine (I was another story). The incident happened in front of a group of people, and once the immediate medical issues were tended to, I felt a defensive heat rise in me. Did they think I was careless or abusive? Were they stripping me of an identity I treasured? For that matter, were they right? How had I let that accident happen? What kind of dog mom was I? With an individual identity I cared about being nibbled away at, I was experiencing self-threat.

In addition to our individual identities, we also have social identities. Psychologists argue that one way we transcend our individual mortality is through the immortality—or at least, continued existence—of the groups to which we belong.[12] These are our social identities. While my individual identities distinguish me from others, my social identities connect me to others. For example, my social identities such as American and person of color are bridges to people like me.[13]

Again, just as with our individual identities, social identities can be threatened.[14] When we feel the groups we belong to are being evaluated negatively, we feel social identity threat. We are naturally drawn to seeing our own groups positively and to craving others to do the same. If someone criticizes professors as out of touch or mothers working outside of the home as cold, I need not believe that they are speaking about me personally to feel social identity threat.

We feel social identity threat because social identities are the remote controls of our minds. When something happens to a member of my group with whom I share a social identity, it triggers an emotional response in me. When an Indian-American kid wins a spelling bee, I glow. When someone from my hometown gets busted for counterfeit sales, I hang my head. While I had nothing to do with the spelling pro or the selling con, my emotions are real. Our social identities are deeply meaningful to who we are and what we care about.

Social identity threat is a cousin of self-threat. When someone critiques me specifically (not just my group), they are saying I am out of touch or I am an inattentive parent. In these instances, I experience self-threat. However, when I am merely a member of the group being critiqued, I identify with the group; by proxy, I feel critiqued. Our social identities tether us to the groups we belong to and care about, for better and for worse.

Our social identity and our history are intertwined. The stories we learn and tell about the past inform our self-conception and sense of our place in the world. One study synthesized the research: "There is a broad consensus across the social sciences that history is an essential ingredient in constructing and maintaining the imagined community of nationhood."[15] We literally define history in national terms like American history, thus linking our social identity to how we capture the past. Another study found that popular history is often a collective memory of conflicts against other groups.[16] What we preserve from the past is a collection of wars, battles, and conflicts between the groups we identify with and the groups we do not identify with. The narrative about those conflicts is grounded in our social identities. How we view the past shapes our identity and our identity shapes how we view the past. Those who share identities also have a shared past. And we often view shared past through the gauzy lens of nostalgia.

Team Nostalgia

Push your way through the endless rainbow of hoodies in either of my teenage daughters' closets and in the far corner, you will find a tiny baby dress as cute as a yawning panda. As I hold those infant frocks with vivid frosting stains, I remember their first birthdays and am swept up in nostalgia about the good ol' days.

Except, those days really were not that good. Yes, our babies were (really) cute and, my goodness, we could not have loved them more. But neither of them slept consistently through the night until they were toddlers (when one did, the other one woke her up). We had two children within thirteen months, both born at least a month early. My physician husband was working long hours on call at the hospital many nights and weekends. I was completing a demanding PhD hundreds of miles away from where my husband worked while applying for highly competitive tenure-track jobs across the country. We had multiple crises in our extended families. Even blessed with above-average resources and flexibility, I was barely hanging on and my hair suddenly started turning gray. I gained thirty pounds that have since made themselves at home and multiplied. We refer to that time period as the Blur and I am happy to barely remember how much of a mess it was.

Still, show me those dresses and I am Team Nostalgia.

What You Want To Hear

Nostalgia, the fond remembrance of one's past, is a sentimental flavor of history. Perhaps we listen to an old song or peruse photos from the past. Perhaps we engage in ancestral rituals or enjoy a story from an elder. Research shows that nostalgic memories lead us to feel more loved and protected, and even more interpersonally competent.[17] Nostalgia creates a sense of belonging and social connection.[18] Our interest in the past is focused on this intimate past, as "almost every American deeply engages the past, and the past that engages them most deeply is that of their family."[19]

Our yearning for nostalgia makes it big business. Movies romanticize the past in gauzy imagery, radio stations spin oldies but goodies, commercials revive classic hits as catchy jingles, advertisers promise the comfort of the good ol' days, and fashion cycles revive bell bottoms and fluorescent patterns. Trend research shows that the "nostalgia pendulum" of pop cultures is a rolling thirty-year cycle, ensuring that everything old will soon be new again.[20] We seek nostalgia on vacation as well, visiting destinations and experiences to connect with people and places of the past. One estimate of global heritage tourism puts the industry at over $1 billion.[21]

When actors Blake Lively and Ryan Reynolds got married in 2012 on a plantation, they fell for nostalgia. The media showered blissful press coverage on the couple. Then, several years later, the internet explained the problem to the bride and groom. Plantations may look pretty and sound romantic, but they were American labor camps. They were built to exploit the land for tobacco and sugar and to exploit enslaved humans for their labor. The owners lived in mansions while the people they enslaved lived in shacks with earthen floors and minimal food rations. Still, weddings at these sites are pitched as romantic affairs, particularly to white clientele. Reynolds later said, "What we saw at the time was a wedding venue on Pinterest. What we saw after was a place built upon devastating tragedy."[22]

In his book *How the Word Is Passed: A Reckoning with the History of Slavery Across America,* Clint Smith describes how some "historical" sites perpetuate fantasies. Smith traveled to former plantations and current prisons, reenactments of Juneteenth and resting places of Confederate soldiers. He wanted to see how slavery is remembered and reckoned with—or not. One tour guide told him, "I think that history is the story of the past, using all the available facts, and that nostalgia is a fantasy about the past using no facts, and somewhere in between is memory, which is kind of this blend of history and a little bit of emotion. . . . I mean, history is kind of about what you need to know . . . but nostalgia is what you want to hear." This theme of nostalgia recurs in many of the sites. Some guides try to feed guests the nostalgia treats they want, while slipping in some truth vegetables. Others just serve dessert, skipping the meal. The guides often mention how the identities of the guests seem to shape their expectations for the site.

Our social identities are central to visits like these, as "the core of a heritage experience lies in the intimate relationship that the person experiences with the heritage."[23] One study found that the extent to which a place relates to one's personal identity predicts one's motivation to visit and one's emotional involvement with the place.[24] As a result, the heritage visit is a "co-creation" in which the "tourist is active rather than passive." The visitor's social identity plugs them into an emotional experience, not just a distant telling of a time long ago.

The joy we find in nostalgia serves a function. Nostalgia bolsters us when we need it most. We yearn most for personal nostalgia when we are lonely or sad and for collective nostalgia—a sentimental longing for one's group's past—when we feel our group's stability is threatened.[25] Nostalgia plays a useful role in protecting our identity and giving us a sense of collective pride. It can lead us to bask in the reflected glory of others.

Basking in Reflected Glory

Psychologist Robert Cialdini had a hunch he could predict what students would wear to class on Mondays. He decided to test his hunch scientifically at universities with big football programs. Cialdini hypothesized that if the football team won over the weekend, students were more likely to wear clothes with the school logo or school colors to class on Monday.

His hunch about the Monday morning effect was right. In fact, if the team won decisively, the effect was even more striking. The students seemed to "bask in reflected glory."[26] Being a fan of a winning team felt like being a "satellite" member of the winning team even if one was not instrumental in the team's success. It was as if the fans' association with the winning team elevated their social status. Such basking in reflected glory as a sports fan is an example of collective pride.[27]

This effect cuts both ways. Research shows that when a team wins, fans are more likely to use *we* and *us* pronouns to refer to the team, and when a team loses, they are more likely to use *they* and *them*. We highlight our connections to victors and hide our connections to losers, or as both George Washington and John F. Kennedy are believed to have said, "Victory has a thousand fathers and defeat is an orphan." This tendency has huge implications for how we view our past and our present. For example, we take pride in Thomas Jefferson's declaration that all men are created equal, while dismissing his track record of enslavement and rape. Because we have not dressed for the weather, emotionally, we are unable to process both wins and losses as our own.

In the United States, collective pride is as American as apple pie. In a study published in 2018, more than 80 percent of Americans reported feeling "extremely" or "very" proud to be an American.[28] We are drawn toward not only the people and history that give us these psychological boosts, but also those who display collective pride. Those who do not display collective pride are seen as betraying the interests of the group.

Of course, national history is an important source of collective pride. When I watch *Finding Your Roots,* I see all the emotional elements of identity, nostalgia, and collective pride. How does one dress for the weather when the past is less positive?

It Comes Alive

To answer this question, I reached out to one of the show's directors and producers, Hazel Gurland-Pooler. Hazel is a white Latina documentary filmmaker. Hazel's love of history bloomed in college, where she was a literature major concentrating in African-American history and gender studies. Her undergraduate thesis was an intersectional examination of African-American journalist Ida B. Wells's antilynching campaign. When we spoke on the phone, she was between calls about the quarantine-stalled filming of a PBS series about the transatlantic slave trade.

Hazel loves both story finding and storytelling. She gets excited as she says, "If you can make an experience from the past feel like an experience that you can understand now, it's much easier. We mythologize the past and it feels so far away and it feels so written in stone. When we get into the visceral stuff, it makes it come alive."

Hazel sees her work as an opportunity to tell untold, unheard stories "that will blow people's minds." When Hazel was starting her career, reality TV was just taking off. It was easier to get that work and it paid better, too. Still, she preferred documentaries, explaining, "History is really revealing. It can be very exciting and entertaining. Documentaries can be stranger than fiction."

On *Finding Your Roots,* these surprises are a centerpiece of the show. Hazel described the goal: "reveal a range of stories—both 'good' and 'bad'—to have dramatic moments, and to reflect the complexity of people's history." White guests "are sometimes terrified" that the show's research team will discover that an ancestor enslaved Africans. "But, of course we will," Hazel explains. "Not because all white people enslaved people, but because if your white ancestors were wealthy enough or worked for someone who was, they're likely going to have a connection to slavery. Because slavery was everywhere; everyone had some connection to it. We don't shy away from the ugly truth. We put it on the guests by asking them, 'How does that make you feel? What do you think you would have done?' "

Of course, negative revelations don't always get "good responses" from guests, Hazel shares. Hazel noticed that the challenging responses were more likely to occur when the story violated a romantic expectation of the guest, such as a traditional Thanksgiving narrative regarding their ancestors' engagement with Native Americans. When it came to the enslavement of African-Americans, guests seem to be less surprised— dressed for the weather, if you will—perhaps reflecting a slightly more accurate understanding of the history of slavery than the genocide of Native Americans.

Hazel knows that "some white people don't want to hear these stories because they're more comfortable or used to a certain history being told." Just as history teacher Jared Urban discovered from his Colorado-born college professor, multiple perspectives are essential to learning history. "But history is almost always told by the conquerors and not by the people who were affected by it or who survived it, who had their community essentially wiped out," says Hazel. She has seen firsthand how our identities affect how we engage with and understand the past, and whether we are ready to face it.

How Not to Be a Superhero

His boyish grin lights up the screen, the way you might expect from a man once named *People* magazine's sexiest man alive as well as the youngest-ever winner of the screenwriting Oscar. Ben Affleck wears a blue button-down shirt and dark blazer, across the table from *Finding Your Roots* host and Harvard University professor Henry Louis Gates Jr. When Gates says, "You are descended from a patriot," Affleck's eyes sparkle. He glances up from a stack of documents to meet Gates's gaze and says, "This is a big surprise! I'm really proud of it."[29]

This now-infamous episode (which Hazel did not work on) received no unusual attention when it aired. But, months later, leaked emails revealed that pride in a patriot ancestor was not all Affleck was feeling. Gates had also shared information about Affleck's slave-owning ancestors. After the taping, Affleck asked that the content not be aired.

His request posed a quandary for the show, one that the producers discussed via email. They decided to accommodate the request by "megastar" and superhero-playing "Batman" Affleck. When word got out, all involved were rebuked for allowing a guest to highlight roots that elicited pride and nostalgia while hiding those that elicited shame.

Eventually, Affleck posted on social media, "I was embarrassed. The very thought left a bad taste in my mouth." He went on to say that he regretted his "initial thoughts that the issue of slavery not be included in the story. We deserve neither credit nor blame for our ancestors and the degree of interest in this story suggests that we are, as a nation, still grappling with the terrible legacy of slavery. It is an examination well worth continuing. I am glad that my story, however indirectly, will contribute to that discussion. While I don't like that the guy is an ancestor, I am happy that aspect of our country's history is being talked about."[30]

I do not know Ben Affleck or his family, nor do I presume to know his specific thoughts and intentions. What I do know is that Affleck is a Hollywood liberal whose nostalgia for his Boston roots and underdog-wins story is well known. He is the American dream, personified. Cue basking in reflected glory. Cue good-guys-win mindset and social identity threat. Cue hindsight bias. Cue collective shame and guilt.

So his response is both relatable and unsurprising. I suspect many—maybe most—of us would have had the same instinct, if not the same megastar clout to dictate reality. I might glow as he did when hearing of the good, and I might want to hide as he did, when hearing about the bad. I might be well prepared for the good weather, and caught off guard by the bad.

Social identity threat does not necessarily need to be about our specific family tree. It can be about any collective identity, including our identity as Americans. Many of us love and deeply identify with our country. Facing its whitewashed past feels like an affront to our American family, even if no one in our biological family was involved or even lived in the country at the time. While no one in my family had ever set foot on American soil before 1968, I still proudly join the standing ovation for World War II veterans at baseball games and I still ran my first (correction: only) marathon in Washington, D.C., to be inspired by the monuments and ideals of our founders as I stumbled to the finish line. Criticize them and you are criticizing me.

Learning about history is as emotional as it is intellectual, maybe more emotional. There is no country nor family without events in its past that disappoint us in the present. In the case of our country, where the facts are indisputable about our whitewashed past, we will surely feel shame, grief, and denial. These natural reactions are the forecast-able emotional weather that we can dress for. Next we will look at what would have helped Affleck when the weather got iffy.

Use Guilt and Shame

The words *guilt* and *shame* are often used interchangeably but the two things actually operate in very specific and distinct ways.[31] Guilt is when I feel like I *did* something bad ("if only I hadn't"), whereas shame is when I feel like I *am* bad ("if only I weren't").[32] Guilt focuses on the impact of our actions on others, while shame focuses on the impact of our actions on how others see us. Guilt is about the action while shame is about the person.

Shame is a particularly painful and incapacitating emotion.[33] Shame sends our brain the message that there is nothing here worth saving. I am bad. I am a bad person. I will be scorned by good people. Shame leaves us with nowhere to go and no way to improve. It makes us want to hide. These messages make us less likely to do the work, not more. In fact, physiological research even shows that our cardiovascular and hormonal systems are activated when we feel shame.[34]

By contrast, when we feel guilt, we are more concerned about the impact of our actions on others. We are less egocentric, and more empathetic, than when we feel shame. The primary advantage of guilt, as opposed to shame, is that when our focus is on our actions, we are more likely to act in a way that makes the problem better, not worse. We are more likely to apologize, confess, and repair harm. We are less likely to avoid the problem.

That said, all is not lost when we feel shame. Psychologists have found that the positive benefits of shame are unlocked when we feel that we can repair the harm.[35] Here is our opportunity to use our tools. If we are focused on whether we can undo the past, then of course we will see no opportunity to repair, as the past is in the past. We will feel shame, we will turn away, we will not reckon with the past. But if we focus on the future, we do have the opportunity for repair, we will not turn away, we will reckon with the past. Shame—like guilt—is useful.

One of the most important ways in which shame is useful is that it helps us know what a society does—and does not—value. In a clever series of studies, behavioral scientists Rebecca Schaumberg and Sam Skowronek tested how study participants responded to seeing facial expressions of shame on others. The study participants not only inferred a group's norms from these nonverbal expressions; they were also less likely to engage in that behavior themselves afterward.[36] Shame, the researchers explain, "broadcasts social norms."

Group-based shame and group-based guilt are the collective parallels to their individual counterparts. Instead of saying "if only I hadn't/wasn't," we are saying "if only we hadn't/weren't" or "if only they hadn't/weren't." The harm was done by others, not by us, but we feel it by virtue of our shared social identity, in the same way that we feel the thrill of victory or the agony of defeat the morning after our favorite team plays. The circumstances that evoke these collective pangs do vary between collective guilt and collective shame.[37] With collective shame, we are most prone when we share and value an identity with those who did the harm. So our pride in our ancestors is fuel for collective shame, which also leads us to distance ourselves from the shame-inducing events.

Interestingly, some distinctions between guilt and shame may be even more distinct when the action was committed by others than when it was committed by ourselves. Both collective guilt and collective shame prime people to repair past harms, a topic we will tackle in a later chapter, but some research finds that group-based guilt is especially likely to generate empathy, as well as motivation to repair and make amends.[38] [39]

In summary, it is appropriate—even useful—to feel shame or guilt about something that hurts others. Shame and guilt reveal what is personally and socially acceptable. When facing our whitewashed past, we might be seduced to think the goal is to avoid guilt or shame, because these emotions feel icky. Affleck did not like how it felt and did not want it amplified publicly.

This avoidance was the problem. Just as we have feelings of pride when we look at the past, we are going to also have feelings of shame and guilt. We need to be ready for the one-two surprise-shame punch.

When we allow for this, we are less likely to be dissuaded by negative emotions. Dressing for the weather means that we are unsurprised when these emotions rain down on us. Shame and guilt can work to our advantage when facing our whitewashed past. The goal is not to avoid them, but to use them.

Allow for Belief Grief

Grief is our response to loss. Sometimes the loss is a loved one who has died or a relationship that has ended. The loss can also be less tangible. In the animated movie *Rise of the Guardians,* starring Chris Pine and Hugh Jackman, the heroes fight to protect the children's belief in Santa Claus, the Tooth Fairy, and the Easter Bunny.[40] I can relate. Like many parents, I have hidden, lied, snuck, and disguised, all in hopes of preventing the loss of a cherished childhood belief. We know that all that stands between the belief and what I call "belief grief" is a spoiler from a tell-all big kid, a scroogey adult, or a stray toy store receipt. Once the word is out, we grieve the loss of what was once true for us.

Few of us have escaped grief in our personal lives but we may not expect grief in the context of beliefs about our country. We expect to grieve the loss of people, relationships, and abilities. Beliefs may feel more internal and eternal. Our beliefs live in our hearts and minds, and when we can no longer hold the beliefs because new information leads us to question and discard them, we experience a loss that I call "belief grief." Belief grief feels awful, like a sad longing and a sharp edge. Like those parents hiding the toys from the kids, we may try to hold on to the outmoded belief a little bit longer, to delay the inevitable grief.

Awful as it feels, grief is functional and must run its course. As we grieve, we shift our relationship from the present to the past and we change how we see ourselves relative to our loss. When we try to suppress or mislabel grief, the negative emotions may spill out in other forms, perhaps anger toward others, or denial and disbelief. Someone once told me that we are doing our best healing when we feel our worst. So as we do the work of facing our whitewashed past, we need to be prepared for the ragged and jagged feeling of belief grief.

Avoid Denial

In his book *States of Denial: Knowing about Atrocities and Suffering,* Stanley Cohen outlines a vast array of ways in which we deny realities, particularly bad realities.[41] He begins the book with a page-long compilation of English language phrases used to describe denial, including turning a blind eye, burying your head in the sand, seeing what you wanted to see, and ignorance is bliss. Whether consciously or unconsciously, maliciously or benevolently, we are prone to denial.

Our tendency toward denial shows up in situations ranging from the personal (denying the impact overeating has on my health) to the interpersonal (denying a loved one's illness) to the societal (denying a friend's racist actions). When it comes to facing our whitewashed past, we may deny that the new information is accurate (despite a preponderance of evidence) or we may deny our ignorance (as if we knew it all along, aka hindsight bias). These denials, while human, reveal that we are focused on protecting ourselves, rather than growing. If we protect and prepare our sense of self in advance, we are less likely to be defensive when faced with information that challenges our beliefs.

A Different Approach

Like Ben Affleck, CNN anchor Anderson Cooper was confronted with ugly news about an ancestor in a different episode of *Finding Your Roots* (again, Hazel did not work on this episode). In front of millions of viewers, he learns that his great-great-great-great-grandfather enslaved twelve people, one of whom eventually killed him. Cooper does not appear defensive. His disgusted reaction to his ancestor's role in slavery seems similar to the reaction he would have had about someone else's ancestor.

I am fascinated by his response, so I tried to learn more. I read Cooper's memoir *The Rainbow Comes and Goes: A Mother and Son on Life, Love, and Loss,* cowritten with his famous-since-childhood mother Gloria Vanderbilt. There he shows the same tendency in reverse, expressing pride in and love for family members without basking in their reflected glory.[42] He holds his collective identity loosely, not abandoning it but also not clinging to it in a way that sends him down the rabbit hole of shame, grief, and denial about facing the past. Somehow he deals with the stormy weather in a way that allows him to stay outside, rather than retreating into a more comfortable, artificially heated space. He seems to have "dressed for the weather."

When we engage with our history without the mindset and tools that allow us to grapple with the tough emotions, we risk a bad or abandoned experience. While I do not know either Anderson Cooper's or Ben Affleck's thoughts and intentions, I suspect there were differences in how they dressed for the weather when facing our and their whitewashed history.

A Self Half Empty

We need to see ourselves as capable, resilient, worthy, and wanted. Whether we do or not will determine whether we see the glass of our self-worth as half empty or half full, and whether we stay with or abandon a challenging task that might poke at our self-worth.

When we—Ben Affleck, Anderson Cooper, you, me—are hit with something that challenges how we want to see ourselves, it shakes us out of our seats at the precise moment when we need to buckle in. This self-threat reflex is especially true on issues of race. Social scientists have found that when white people feel self-threat about their whiteness—as

Affleck might have—they usually adopt one of three strategies.[43] They deny racism, or they distance themselves from others implicated in the racism, or they try to address the issue by working to dismantle the racism. Neither denying nor distancing is useful when it comes to reckoning with racism, but both strategies are tempting to alleviate the difficult emotions. What we really want to do is adopt that third strategy of dismantling the systems that have spilled into the present from the past. To do this, we need our self-worth to be half full.

Flex Your Self

Thankfully, we can rely on the flexibility of what psychologists call our "self-system" or what I sometimes call our "flex self." Our flex self adapts to threats by using whatever is available to protect itself. In particular, studies show that helping people connect to something larger than themselves can be powerful.[44] A reminder of what we care about, beyond our own ego and self-image, leads to a drop in defensiveness when something threatens that ego or self-image.[45] A fairly simple intervention of "values affirmation" can bolster our sense of self and give us the protection we need to deal with threats to our sense of self days, weeks, months, and maybe even years later. We become less defensive to threatening information when we have had this boost in advance.

Consider this classic study.[46] Seventh-grade students of different races attended a school with a racial achievement gap in which white students consistently had higher GPAs than black and Hispanic students. The students completed occasional reflection and writing prompts focused on the things most important to them (relationships with friends, with family, personal interests) for about fifteen minutes. As a parent, I suspect these seventh graders did not consciously think too much about these reflection activities afterward.

Over the next two years, the students encountered highs and low as they navigated schoolwork, teachers, families, friends, and, particularly for the black and Hispanic students, stereotypes, biases, and structural barriers. Setbacks were inevitable and they might have easily succumbed to a defeatist narrative.

Unbeknownst to them, the exercises were designed to be a booster shot during these exact moments of challenge. "Values affirmation," particularly at critical moments (for example, beginning of school year, prior to tests, near the holiday season), shifts the baseline of how individuals see themselves, creating a more solid return state when there is psychological threat. Self-threat becomes less threatening.

To measure the impact of values affirmation, researchers tracked those students over the following two years. The intervention reduced the racial achievement gap by 30 percent. Black—not white—students saw a boost. The worst-performing students benefited the most. White students showed no difference. Researcher Geoffrey Cohen explains: "It's clear that broadening their perspective on themselves reduces minority students' sense of threat and therefore the likeliness that they will falter."[47]

While this finding has been replicated in other academic contexts in which a group is stereotyped and under self-threat (for example, female students in physics),[48] the academic context and stereotypes are not the larger point. The context might be a newly merged company in which employees of the acquired firm wrestle with external and internal critiques. To maintain their performance in the face of these threats, they might each revisit their core values in a personal reflection and writing activity. The larger point is that affirming our values makes it easier for us to lift ourselves out of the anxieties and emotions that stem from external stereotypes and internal doubts.

Behavioral scientists have even found that prosocial behavior—like helping a colleague at work or donating money to charity—is constrained by worries people have about themselves.[49] When study participants completed a values affirmation task in which they picked from a list of values (for example, forgiveness, honesty, kindness) and wrote about why these values mattered to them, prosocial behavior increased as a function of their greater self-regard.

To recap, values affirmation can help us remain resilient when threatened, whether we face self-threat or social identity threat. When we are unlearning our country's whitewashed past, such resilience is important, as we will feel threatened. We will need that booster shot and a more robust baseline, as the next study shows.

Another Layer of Protection

Researchers have extended research on values affirmation at the individual level to the collective level, where we struggle with social identity threat.[50] In a series of studies, conducted more than a decade before the recent news that the remains of hundreds of indigenous children were found at the former sites of residential "schools," they tested the affirmation strategy. In Canada, as in the United States, children of indigenous families were removed through threats or force from their families' homes with the promise of an education. In reality, abuse was widespread and the children were forbidden from speaking their native language. Even after the children died from abuse and neglect, their remains were not returned to their families.

In these values affirmation studies, researchers recruited Canadians (of non-Aboriginal descent) and had them read this defensiveness-prompting, truth-telling paragraph.

By the early twentieth century, Canada had come to view Aboriginals' "savage" way of life as a threat to "civilized" society. . . . As a consequence, thousands of Aboriginal children were removed, often forcibly, from their families and communities and shipped hundreds of miles to residential schools. . . . Although the Aboriginal communities had been promised that their youth would be educated, the children were typically not allowed to progress past a grade three education. . . . Instead of preparing Aboriginal children to be productive members of society, Canada's real aim was to "kill the Indian in the child" by destroying their sense of Aboriginal culture and identity. . . . [T]hey were prohibited from speaking Aboriginal languages or practicing Aboriginal rituals. Those caught doing so, even if only amongst themselves, were more often than not severely beaten. . . . [S]qualid living conditions led to rampant disease and death. Although ignored by government officials and public alike, mortality rates in these schools ranged from 35% to 60%. . . . [T]here were over 50,000 deaths and another 91,000 reports of physical, emotional, and sexual abuse.

The key is what the participants did before reading this paragraph. They were all presented with a list of twelve values. Half of the participants selected and wrote about the value they believed to be most important to Canadians; the other half selected and wrote about the value they believed to be least important to Canadians generally.

It worked. The value-affirmed participants felt less defensive, which is good. Essentially, they were vaccinated with affirmations before the threat hit. They also felt more collective guilt and collective shame, which does not feel good but is a necessary step toward taking responsibility,* offering a path toward facing our whitewashed history.

Not only are values affirmations small in scale and large in impact; they do not even enter people's consciousness in a meaningful way. People likely do not attribute their resilience to the cheesy exercise they did last year. Imagine someone tuned up your bike without telling you and you found yourself turning corners more easily and hitting the brakes more confidently, without realizing how or why. Or, perhaps, without realizing anything was happening.

Perhaps Anderson Cooper was better dressed for the weather than Ben Affleck, ready for the emotions and equipped to deal with them rather than retreat. When we are taking on a new challenge, such as learning about history in which our ancestors did harm to others, we

---

*For our purposes here, the distinction between collective guilt and collective shame is less important than the value of both collective guilt and collective shame.

may feel understandably threatened. Whether we sink or rise to the moment may rest in how connected we are to our own values. We can dress for the weather by considering the values we hold dear, thus being better prepared for an onslaught of shame, grief, and denial.

The Forecast Is Usually Wrong

Self-threat is tough to handle in the present and even tougher when forecast for the future. Our minds guard against whatever makes us feel bad, convincing us to abandon the task we planned to do. When we forecast stormy weather ahead, we might not leave the house.

These emotional forecasts impact all of our decisions—whether to quit that job or move in with that partner or watch that show. When our forecasts are wrong, we might overcorrect in our decisions. I bet that is what happened with Affleck.

Unfortunately, we are not reliable emotional meteorologists. Research shows that human beings do a poor job predicting how they will feel about a particular situation in the future. We overestimate how happy good things—like winning the lottery—will make us feel and how sad bad things—like a terrible accident—will make us feel. Psychologist Daniel Gilbert refers to this prediction process of how we will feel (our "affect") in the future as "affective forecasting."[51] He and his colleagues find that we are reasonably accurate in predicting what will feel positive and what will feel negative. That is, we are good at distinguishing between a root beer and a root canal. We lose accuracy in our predictions about how long we will feel that emotion and at what intensity. We think the root beer will feel better and for longer than it does and we think the root canal will feel worse and for longer than it does. Our minds (and those of movie stars) overdramatize things.

We miscalculate in part because we do not take into account how good we are at making sense of things. We constantly incorporate new experiences into our understanding of the world. We stretch our understanding like a pair of jeans and that "sense making" loosens up whatever intensity we were feeling, creating a more comfortable fit, closer to our baseline. In fact, we are motivated to make sense of things, and the wackier the thing, the greater our (unconscious) motivation to make it fit in (much like the system justifying a good-guys-win mindset). Soon the thing that loomed so large and extreme in our forecast becomes normalized into our daily experience, and even seems inevitable because of our hindsight bias.

We have seen this in vivid terms during the pandemic, during which working from home, wearing a mask, and dining outdoors in the winter have morphed from unfathomable to unremarkable. When Affleck's story came out, he took far more flack for the cover-up than for his family tree. He got the forecast wrong, overestimating how unbearable it would be to reckon with the truth.

This is no accident. Psychologists Timothy Wilson and Daniel Gilbert write, "Like the physiological immune system that fights threats to physical health, people have a psychological immune system that fights threats to emotional well-being." Just like our physiological immune system, our psychological immune system works mostly outside our awareness, finding and fighting off threats without requiring us to make a conscious effort.

Our forecast is likely off when it comes to unlearning whitewashed American history. We forecast a torrential storm when the reality is more like a short downpour that clears into a beautiful blue sky. No doubt, we will need to dress for the weather and bring an umbrella, but we need not turn around.

While Gilbert and colleagues have had little success trying to improve the accuracy of people's emotional forecasts, they do have a solution to the bad forecast problem. The best way to improve our forecasts is simply not to forecast how we will feel, but rather to ask other people—friends or even strangers—how *they* think we will feel. Gilbert and colleagues even find that people are even better off relying on the experience of a single randomly selected stranger than on themselves.[52] This insight suggests that reading about, listening to, and talking to people who have gone down the path of facing our country's whitewashed past may be useful.

In Anderson Cooper's voice, I hear love of family and love of country, while he stares atrocity in the eye rather than denying it. The title of his book refers to a rainbow that comes and goes, and perhaps that is a metaphor for his approach. He is ready for the highs and lows. It is refreshing, almost startling, to hear someone speak about their family with an air of objectivity that is not coldness nor distance, just an ability to put aside shame, guilt, and denial. For days after I finished listening to Cooper's narration of his audiobook, I kept hearing his calming voice in my mind. He reckoned with the past without sacrificing love. Surely we can do this as well.

In Part A, we have sized up the unlearning we need to do as we determine where to start. My trainer, Meghan, illustrated the importance of seeing the problem, while Ben Affleck and Anderson Cooper offered a contrast in dressing for the stormy weather of unlearning. Next, in Part B, we tackle what to do and how the tools of embracing paradox, connecting the dots, and rejecting fables can help us.

Part B

What Do
We Do?

Embrace Paradox

How wonderful that we have met with a paradox.
Now we have some hope of making progress.
—NIELS BOHR

Juneteenth

To the dismay of my husband and kids, I do not use an iPhone. I am proud to be on Team Android, though for a moment in 2018 I felt out of the loop. That year, unbeknownst to me, the iPhone calendar denoted June 19 as Juneteenth for the first time. When this came to my attention, I was already writing an article about the holiday for my monthly *Forbes* column. Juneteenth has long commemorated the end of slavery but I had somehow belatedly learned about the holiday on the internet. The gist of my planned piece was "I was today years old when I realized that July 4 was a day of independence in name but not practice."

Seriously, how had I not noticed that 1776 (the birth of our nation) and 1865 (the end of the Civil War) were almost a century apart? It wasn't until almost one hundred years after the signing of the Declaration of Independence that the Emancipation Proclamation began to eliminate slavery in most states, and then it was more than two years after that when the change was actually communicated to all who were enslaved.[1] Independence Day is a poorly and ironically named holiday.

The unexpected appearance of Juneteenth on everyone's iPhones deepened my worry that I was the last person to know. Embarrassed, I debated whether I should even write the piece. On the one hand, I felt like I was revealing a performative interest in justice that was unsupported by my knowledge. On the other hand, I felt like I was peeing in the patriotic pool by challenging our love affair with Independence Day. I wondered if I could love my country while questioning the day whose very essence is love of country.

To fish for validation—I mean, information—I posted a query on social media. Who knew what Juneteenth was, without googling? Who celebrated the day and if so, how? The nonscientific results of my poll were fascinating. The odds of someone knowing about the day increased if they lived in Texas (where the holiday originated) and/or were black and/or watched television shows that center on black characters like *Atlanta* and *Black-ish* (I watch *Black-ish* but had missed the Juneteenth episode). The poll made me feel better because I was definitely not the only one, but it also made me feel worse. Why were so many of us so unaware?

Considered as a pair, Independence Day and Juneteenth reveal our nation's complicated, contradictory history. July 4 celebrates our purported ideals, sidelining our wrongs. June 19 celebrates our wrongs belatedly corrected to match our ideals. Together the two holidays epitomize our national—and human—condition: living in paradox. To be a patriot of this country is to learn to live with paradox.

What Is Paradox?

We encounter paradox throughout our daily lives. A paradox exists when two opposing statements are both true, creating an absurd contradiction. We know walking is more active than standing *and* that standing can be more tiring than walking. Both things are true, though seemingly at odds. Many ancient traditions—such as the Chinese philosophy of yin and yang—encourage us to embrace paradox. Core scientific breakthroughs of the past century—relativity theory, quantum theory, chaos theory, and complexity theory—have upended either/or, right/wrong assumptions in our understanding of how the physical world works, suggesting that while our minds expect consistency, the world does not actually operate that way.

Despite the fact that paradox persists in our daily lives and has existed in the human experience for millennia, human beings crave the opposite—consistency and coherence. Both consciously and unconsciously, our minds react to cognitive inconsistencies as if they were crooked pictures on the wall. We want to nudge them into place, and when we cannot or do not, we cringe. We try to align our thoughts with each other, and align our thoughts with our actions, and align our actions today with our actions yesterday. When they do not line up, we experience discomfort, embarrassment, guilt, or the need to justify the inconsistency. Remember what happens when the past and present do not feel continuous? We amp up our identity. We are skilled at creating the semblance of consistency and the illusion of a pattern, as a means of dealing with these feelings.

This need for consistency is a foundational finding in the study of human behavior, often serving as the underlying mechanism in a wide range of psychological theories about balance, congruence, linearity, and rationality. One example is the "binary bias," our tendency to flatten complex stories into simple either/or binaries.[2] We look at Yelp reviews that span the 1–5 scale and flatten the conclusion into either a thumbs-up or thumbs-down. We hear a nuanced approach to solving a big problem in society and extract that the approach is either brilliant or ignorant. We see someone behave differently in different contexts and conclude they are either hero or villain. The binary bias makes it difficult to allow for paradox.

Consistency Cravings

Even compared to others' craving for consistency, I suspect my compulsion for consistency runs a tad deeper. I cannot understand how my teenage daughter watches episodes of *Brooklyn 99* randomly, not sequentially. I am still unsettled by a recent blue ink entry I accidentally added in my planner, where I *always* write with a black pen. I use a slash when referring to my husband's and my different last names together, while my husband sometimes uses a hyphen and sometimes a slash (I love him, so we are still married despite the inconsistent punctuation situation). Seriously, I challenge anyone to a consistency-craving battle. While you may not be quite as compulsive, chances are that you have the normal human craving for coherence.

It is also equally normal that human beings are complex, that human behavior varies more by situation than by person, and that human psychology is fraught with contradiction. The kicker is that we not only crave consistency, we are under the illusion that we (and others) are consistent. We categorize ourselves; perhaps we are a "casual type" or a "people person" or a "go-getter." But put us in a situation at work where we want to impress a client or boss, and we may be styling our hair and wearing our Sunday best, not appearing at all casual. If we do not fit in or feel comfortable with our colleagues, we may choose to eat lunch at our desks, thus appearing to be more of a loner than a people person. And, if we feel our work efforts are repeatedly diminished and disrespected, we might slouch into a slacker mindset. Context shapes behavior. Still, we tend to see ourselves and others through the lens of consistency.

Remember system justification theory—the good-guys-win mindset we discussed in my story about the little house on the prairie? This need to see the systems around us as good is another example of our consistency craving. The injustices of the world are inconsistencies. One way to resolve these inconsistencies is to reframe them as just. It gives us a greater sense of security, certainty, and belonging. Our minds wiggle into consistency in the most acrobatic ways.

Ironically, humans crave consistency yet rarely behave consistently or find consistency in others. People are complicated, defying narratives of being all good or all bad. True, different people can experience, see, and remember the same event completely differently. True, our ancestors did both honorable and horrible things. True, our wealth today came from hard work and theft from others. True, this land is our land and this land was their land. All of it is true. Little of it is consistent. And we need to embrace that paradox.

A Big Asterisk

I eventually wrote two articles about Juneteenth. The first was that *Forbes* piece, which went semiviral in 2018 because apparently many people googled the unfamiliar holiday when it appeared on their iPhone calendars. My piece was one of the first hits that came up. In 2021, I wrote a second piece in my *Dear Good People* newsletter.[3] By then everyone knew Juneteenth and I shifted my focus from explaining the holiday to explaining how *not* to commemorate it (for example, symbols are essential for change but don't confuse symbols with change).

Both pieces attracted more attention than usual, suggesting that many people are grappling with our national paradox: a country of egalitarian ideals founded on slavery. In 2018 I wrote:

> White America is celebrating 242 years of freedom this year. Black America is celebrating only 153 years of freedom from actually being held captive, bought and sold by their fellow Americans, and not even 60 years of freedom from legalized segregation. Sixty years is a blink of an eye when it comes to economic progress and attitude change. We still enjoy TV shows, movies and music that are older than the end of segregation. We still live in houses and apartment buildings that are older than the end of segregation. We still have family who are older than the end of segregation. In fact, the first African-Americans to integrate segregated schools are barely old enough to qualify for Social Security benefits—that is how recent our past is.[4]

In sports, when a record is set or a championship is won, and later deemed illegitimate, officials must decide how to note the anomaly. Rather than erase the original accomplishment from the record books, the solution is often to add a qualifying asterisk. The asterisked feat becomes a stain, a scarlet letter, a badge of dishonor.

Just as we cannot accept Lance Armstrong's Tour de France winning streak without question or Barry Bonds's home run record without a footnote, we cannot accept American history at face value without an asterisk. July 4 needs an asterisk. That asterisk signals a "certain terms and conditions may apply" caveat to the celebration of independence. While an asterisk might seem like puny punctuation, its symbolic role is mighty. The asterisk says that there is some unlearning to do. What you thought you knew was both true and untrue.

In some ways, this book was born with that Juneteenth piece. It was one of the first times when I faced the depth of my whitewashed understanding of American history, and the emotional difficulty of reckoning with that. Writing about Juneteenth hit every nerve, every hot button, every trigger. I was not as smart or as engaged as a citizen, as in tune with the times, as strong of an ally as I thought I was. I was not even as good a person as I thought I was. The more I learned, the more asterisks I saw and the less equipped I felt to handle them. That asterisk, I now realize, is the punctuation of paradox.

Here is where I landed. We should wear red, white, and blue on both days. We should celebrate our progress on June 19 and commit again to our ideals on July 4. June 19 celebrates our attempts to do better and July 4 celebrates how we should have been better all along. To celebrate only July 4 is to reject paradox in favor of the fable that was never a reality. To celebrate only June 19 is to miss the opportunity to remind us of our ideals. Most of all, we will need tools to embrace contradiction and paradox to reckon with our whitewashed history.

"Without a Second Thought"

Talking to Mitch is a shot of adrenaline. He loves the "great American city" of New Orleans, in which he grew up, perhaps more than most people love their cities (and I am writing this from New York City, whose residents are hard to beat when it comes to love of city). He loves its history and he loves its people. His enthusiasm for its history and people is contagious. And it runs in the family; generations of Mitch's family have been active as community volunteers and in the local government.

After the devastation of Hurricane Katrina in 2005 on his "historic, beautiful, deeply rich city," Mitch poured himself into the rebuilding effort. In that effort, he reached out to an old friend, who was quick to sign on. But he surprised Mitch by asking for something in return—support for the removal of Confederate monuments from prominent places. Mitch remembers being surprised by the request.

"Though I grew up in one of New Orleans' most diverse neighborhoods, I must have passed by those monuments a million times without giving them a second thought," Mitch told me. He was not alone. Likely millions of others did the same every year. Still, some noticed and those who did were probably disproportionately affected in negative ways by racism.

It wasn't that Mitch had never thought about racism in his city, which was once one of America's largest human trafficking (slave) markets.

In fact, the opposite was true. His white family's "long, proud history of fighting for civil rights" once even led to a white woman saying she wanted to kill young Mitch because his father was a "[racial epithet] lover." He cared deeply about equality. Still, the statues he walked by were not at the top of his mind as his city struggled in the aftermath of Katrina.

These statues were products of the Cult of the Lost Cause's rebranding of the city's history and rewriting of history. The three statues were of Robert E. Lee (the Confederate general who led the South's attempt to secede from the United States), Jefferson Davis (president of the Confederate States of America during the Civil War), and Pierre Gustave Toutant Beauregard (a prominent Confederate general). The fourth was a monument honoring the White League, a post–Civil War organization of racist militants.

Some claim the Confederacy has nothing to do with racism, arguing it is more about nostalgia for a time period, a place, a feeling, and a culture. This view ignores pointed and ugly facts. It is unambiguous that the Confederacy was founded on racist ideals. The vice president of the Confederacy, Alexander Stephens, said in a famous 1861 speech to justify secession that the Confederacy's "corner-stone rests upon a great truth, that the negro is not equal to the white man; that slavery—subordination to the superior race—is his natural and normal condition. This, our new government, is the first, in the history of the world, based upon this great physical, philosophical, and moral truth."[5] The cornerstone of the Confederacy and the cornerstone of the monuments was "subordination to the superior race." The nostalgia is for formal and informal systems soaked in that Confederacy.

Mitch became convinced that change was long overdue. The Confederate monuments needed to go. His friend from lunch—the Pulitzer Prize– and Grammy Award–winning musician Wynton Marsalis—was right. And Mitch—aka New Orleans mayor Mitch Landrieu—needed to lead the effort.

"Living in a Contradiction"

In his book, *In the Shadow of Statues: A White Southerner Confronts History,* Mayor Landrieu describes the effort in which he mobilized the legislative, judicial, and executive branches of government in New Orleans to garner the political, legal, and popular standing to remove the Confederate monuments.[6] It took all his political will and skill to make it happen, and some say he gambled his career. In the end, it required gut-wrenching debate, public hearings, multiple commissions, votes by the City Council, and review by thirteen different federal and state judges. Landrieu struggled to find a construction company willing to rent out a crane for the controversial undertaking and when he finally did, he had to conceal the identities of the crane operators to protect them from backlash. It is difficult to imagine another mayoral action about use of a public space requiring such an intense effort.

Still, Landrieu was determined. As the statues came down, he stood at a podium nearby, giving remarks that would soon go viral: "To literally put the Confederacy on a pedestal in our most prominent places of honor is an inaccurate recitation of our full past, it is an affront to our present, and it is a bad prescription for our future."

Now, a few years later, I was on the phone with the former mayor while the pandemic raged in the background of both of our lives and cities. I expected to hear fiery words about tearing things down. Instead I was struck by the juxtaposition of his comments about tearing things down and building things up. I was confused about his conspicuous love of his city paired with his determination to reject some of the city's history and the will of some of the city's people. I asked him to explain.

Without hesitation, he responded, "Most of the time, we're living in a contradiction." That's when I realized that Mayor Mitch Landrieu has mastered the paradox mindset.

Paradox Mindset

In their book, *Both/And Thinking: Embracing Creative Tensions to Solve Your Toughest Problems,* management professors Wendy Smith and Marianne Lewis are inspired by the tenet that "the problem is not the problem; the problem is the way we think about the problem."[7] They argue that our need for consistency need not be a problem, if we can allow our brains to find consistency in the inconsistency. For example, it is not inconsistent that a people person eats lunch at their desk and a casual person dresses up at work, when one remembers the power of the situation in shaping behavior. What looks inconsistent is actually very consistent.

To find consistency in inconsistency, Smith and Lewis suggest a "paradox mindset." In this mindset, we do not keep looking for the missing puzzle piece; we simply accept that the puzzle is unsolvable. We "live in the absurdity" of the unsolvable puzzle, just as Mayor Landrieu seems to do, rather than getting bogged down in the absurdity. This is good news that there is hope for humans who like consistency, even consistency junkies like me.

A paradox mindset has been found to develop with age and challenging experiences, as individuals navigate the tensions of life, which means every one of us has paradox mindset momentum in our aging favor.[8] Even better, a paradox mindset can be learned[9] and prompted by others, just by telling people to hold two opposing ideas simultaneously.[10] The mindset may also have a physiological and neurological basis.[11]

In the early years of graduate school, before she was a leading paradox expert, Wendy and I shared an office. I sometimes joined her for morning runs before we parked ourselves at our computers. Years later, I was eager for her wise take. I wondered if she would confirm my discovery of a paradox mindset in the wild.

When I reach Wendy, she is on a writer's retreat in a cabin in the woods, literally writing about how to use the paradox mindset—also known as both/and thinking—to solve tough problems in the real world. I tell her about my interview and share some quotes. She gets excited. "I definitely hear both/and thinking," she exclaims. She rattles off the paradox mindset tools she notices.

First, Wendy notes that Mayor Landrieu accepts that tensions between two opposing forces, or dualities, are a natural state. "We all live in some semblance of a duality all the time. It's almost constant," he had told me. This comfort, as Smith and Lewis call it, allows him to unclench his shoulders, take a deep breath, and deal with reality. Wendy and her coauthor Ella Miron-Spektor have written about the analogy of adolescents' argumentative temperaments. Such behavior can be disconcerting and upsetting to the parent or caregiver, especially when the behavior is new. However, if parents can reframe teenage storminess as developmentally appropriate, it lands differently. It is still disconcerting and upsetting at times (speaking from real-time experience here), but there is less mental pull to make the new behavior align with the old. Comfort makes us, well, more comfortable with the paradox.

Next, Wendy explains, Mayor Landrieu shifts the question from "is this bad thing true or is this good thing true?" to "in what ways can this good thing be true?" For example, instead of asking himself and others an either/or question like "Is New Orleans built on a foundation of greatness or a foundation of racism?" he asks, "What is great about this city?" Instead of asking "What are we going to tear down or save?" he asks, "What are we going to build back in New Orleans?" Instead of "Do you or don't you love your country?" he asks, "What does it mean to love your country?" Releasing the either/or assumption, as Smith and Lewis call it, allows for active exploration of how our actions might shape the truth, without getting bogged down in binaries.

Third, changing questions is not a free-for-all or a panacea. Real differences between opposing demands do exist. Boundaries bring structure to paradox. Embracing paradox does not lead to a free-for-all where everything can be both true and untrue. For example, Mayor Landrieu's overall vision involved tapping into our highest and best selves as people and as a city, and that meant taking care of each other. This vision of a city where people take care of each other might serve as a boundary within which he can explore paradox. Contradictions can exist, within these boundaries.

Finally, Wendy notes that the paradox mindset is dynamic. Things change. We see this dynamic approach in Mayor Landrieu. His paradox mindset was strong, and yet he had been walking past the monuments without processing the contradiction of their presence. When he spoke with Marsalis, his thinking evolved. As he told me, "What else is there that I walk by every day and don't notice and don't understand? You get quickly to the issue of institutional bias and racism that we walk by every day and don't notice. Like the neighborhoods that we live in that are cordoned off from other neighborhoods by transportation systems that stop at suburbia, a criminal justice system that puts people in jail and says, 'You can't get out unless you pay cash bail,' redlining, the whole nine yards." His mind had the capacity to iterate into considering other contradictions. When embracing paradox, our understanding will be dynamic.

These four tips about assumptions, boundaries, comfort, and dynamic approaches are what Smith and Lewis call the ABCD framework. Together they make it easier to put on that paradox mindset that Landrieu seems to wear.

When reckoning with our whitewashed history, there is little ambiguity about whether or not paradox exists. It does. It is clear as a sunny Independence Day in the primary documents of American history. This reckoning is not a prospecting-mission dig for gold, where we might or might not find gold. Rather, this is an Easter egg hunt. The eggs are there—we just need to find them. The question is just whether we are looking hard enough and in the right places.

What Becomes Possible

Research shows that we have much to gain from embracing the ABCDs of a paradox mindset. It can enable resilience[12] and lead to more creativity.[13] These positive outcomes make sense, as we are no longer burning mental fuel trying to solve unsolvable problems or giving up prematurely because we cannot see a path forward. Rather than agonizing over whether to celebrate a holiday, we educate ourselves and update our traditions. Rather than ignoring feedback about an established term in our industry, we upgrade our lingo to reflect the ethos of the times and shed what is not serving us. We persist, we cope, and we innovate.

While writing this book during a global pandemic, violent insurrection, and rising extremism, I have tied myself in a knot multiple times trying to make sense of my beliefs. People are fundamentally good . . . or are they? The world is making progress . . . or is it? Democracy will prevail . . . or will it? In each of these quandaries, I seemed intent on answering a multiple-choice question with no option to respond "all of the above."

Sometimes the answer is "all of the above." When we release the need to solve an unsolvable problem, we shed a heavy, clumsy load of anxiety and discomfort. The tension of trying to resolve a paradox can be emotionally depleting[14] and that energy can be released for other cognitive and emotional tasks.[15] We also see new possibilities. The world is complicated and nuanced. It takes effort to see beneath the surface. When we do, however, new possibilities emerge. People are both good and bad, and situations will shape their behavior more than we realize. The world is making progress, but it is not always linear. Democracy can prevail, but only if we fight for it. The paradox mindset and these resulting insights give us agency we lack when we put ourselves in a tight either/or corner.

The constant need to make sense of something will lead us to plummet into an either/or solution, whether or not the solution is correct, just to ease the strain. It would be like deciding on where to vacation based on when your suitcase felt too heavy to carry anymore, as opposed to selecting a destination that suited your needs.

Best of all, we develop skills that have benefits beyond the issue at hand, such as learning, agility, cognitive flexibility,[16] openness to experiences, tolerance for ambiguity, and complex thinking, all skills correlated with or arising from a paradox mindset. We become better at thinking in different ways, which is useful in many contexts. In fact, this ability to embrace paradox has been found to be an important coping mechanism for life's challenges, with evidence that people who have dealt with complicated life experiences such as divorce or trauma show better skills in this area.

Mayor Landrieu's story shows us that new possibilities emerge when we get better at activating our paradox mindset. We can remind ourselves of how Landrieu's monument project began—he was leading his city's rebuilding efforts in a city still devastated by Hurricane Katrina, years later, and was asking Marsalis for help. Seemingly out of the blue, Marsalis brought up an issue that predated Katrina—the monuments. It is easy to imagine that Landrieu might have compartmentalized these issues. First priority—post-Katrina recovery. Later priority—monument removal. Such intuitive prioritization would be the natural result of either/or thinking.

However, with both/and thinking, he was able to integrate these issues. Rather than isolating racism from hurricane recovery, he saw the overarching questions that united both issues. Neither was happening in isolation. Landrieu was considering everything from the buildings to the people to the culture, and asking, "What are we going to build back?" He took an "introspective dive about who we were (before Katrina) and who we wanted to be (after Katrina)." The monuments were "just one very, very, very small part" of helping New Orleans find its way to being a "great American city by holding on to the good parts of our past, letting go of the bad parts, and then preparing people and giving them the tools that they needed to have a beautiful and a wonderful future." Not everyone bought in, but many did.

Eventually this rebuilding effort led to Landrieu being named "Public Official of the Year" by *Governing* in 2015 and "America's top turnaround mayor" in 2016 by a *Politico* survey of American mayors.[17] In his May 23, 2017, speech about the monument removal, he said, "For America and New Orleans, it has been a long, winding road, marked by great tragedy and great triumph." He sees a future where we can *both* love this country *and* critique it, where we *both* honor our past *and* be honest about it. He sees paradox as full of possibility.

Paradox Spotting

When our kids were young, we started a silly travel tradition called "adventure points." As we set out on a road trip or a flight, we would say, "Get as many points as you can today, kids!" Took a wrong turn? Adventure point! Can't find a restroom? Another point! Flight delay? Points! Feeling motion sick? Double points! All the misadventures on our adventures added up.

While born of maternal desperation when the kids were young and our plane was struck by lightning (all was fine, but yikes), the approach was backed up by robust psychological research. First, it reset the reference point from being "everything goes right" to "some things go wrong," and second, it reframed our work to be noticers. The paradox mindset is essentially the same thing: a quest for paradox points, a challenge to become an expert paradox spotter, even paradox chaser.

Mitch Landrieu says, "You're always going to have this tension between valuing history and valuing progress. You're always going to have this tension between history being painful and history being prideful. It's just never going to go away." In this case, we are better off with a reference point that equips us for paradox and nudges us toward a positive emotional experience. Our history is as rich as it is flawed.

These positive emotions allow us to navigate paradox more effectively.[18] Imagine paradox being associated with gratitude, pride, and joy. For example, when I think about the paradox of racism in the workplace, I am struck both by legal advances that make discrimination more difficult and by the clear lack of progress in diversifying the senior positions in many organizations. Because both things are true, I might sink into confusion and inertia. Or I might feel gratitude for the recognition, pride in my growing awareness, and joy in the evidence of the possibility of improvement.

As a consistency fiend, my mental workaround is simple. Consistently expect inconsistency (and the potential disappointment). Once I accepted that, I could more easily accept ink changes in my planner, nonsequential episodes in my show, punctuation discrepancies in my return address . . . and paradoxes in the history of this country. Changing our frame of reference from expecting consistency to expecting inconsistency will help us spot paradox.

It is also useful to have a mental fail-safe mechanism. When our paradox mindset begins to malfunction, leading us back to the dangerous binary, a metaphor or catchphrase can keep us safe from this-or-that thinking. Perhaps it is a rose, full of both beautiful flowers and painful thorns. Perhaps it is a catchphrase like "both/and" or "yes and." These quick, memorable mental tools can reactivate our paradox mindset.

Additionally, we can step outside of our situation. Wendy reveals a pro tip: "When I teach about the paradox mindset in group workshops, I find people are able to find both/and in other people's situations much quicker than they can find a both/and in their own situation." When we are struggling to see the paradox in America, perhaps we can run the thought experiment that it is a different country that holds these contradictions. With less at stake in terms of our own identity, we may be better able to embrace paradox.

As we wrap up our call, Wendy reminds me that embracing paradox is "not for the faint of heart." Got it, I say. That is okay, this is the land of the brave. Americans take pride in our strength. If paradox spotting is for the strong, then we are just the people to take it on. Once we learn to see the problem like Meghan Lydon, dress for the weather like Anderson Cooper, and embrace paradox like Mayor Mitch Landrieu, we will be better able to connect whitewashed dots between the past and the present. We tackle those next.

Connect the Dots

The distinction between past, present,
and future is only a stubbornly persistent illusion.
—ALBERT EINSTEIN

It's Not Ancient History

On the overcast fall day, four bell ringers stood ready. On cue, they pulled the rope—and our heartstrings. The bell sang its origin story: a secret black church founded by enslaved people under a grove of trees in Virginia in 1776, only to be hidden centuries later under a parking lot in Colonial Williamsburg. The rope connected the past and future, wrapped in the fingers of the first black president and the first black First Lady of the United States (she, a descendant of enslaved people), and those of seven-year-old Christine and her family elder, ninety-nine-year-old Ruth Bonner. Bonner clasped the rope with aged yet determined fingers, no doubt remembering her father, Elijah Odom, who was born into slavery. They were ringing the bell to commemorate the opening of the National Museum of African American History and Culture, led by Lonnie Bunch, the first African-American and first historian head of the Smithsonian Institution.

The hands pulled, the bell rang, the tears flowed, and the dots connected between Elijah, Ruth, and Christine, past and present. At that event, President Obama said, "It [this new museum] reminds us that routine discrimination and Jim Crow aren't ancient history, it's just a blink in the eye of history. It was just yesterday. And so, we should not be surprised that not all the healing is done. We shouldn't despair that it's not all solved."

In 2016 when they rang that bell and in 2022 as I write, people still have parents—or grandparents, great-grandparents, or great-great-grandparents—who were enslaved. There is a trivial amount of generational time connecting these seemingly unrelated dots that some of us (I) had mistakenly misfiled in a mental folder labeled "a long time ago." Slavery was not so long ago.

I also thought of desegregation as taking place a long time ago. I picture that iconic Norman Rockwell painting featuring Ruby Bridges, a black elementary school student in a white frock carrying her school supplies. Zooming in on her, she looks like any six-year-old dressed with care by people who love her as she heads to the first day of school. But, looking at the whole image, we see that she is escorted by four towering uniformed deputy U.S. marshals who protect her from violent opponents of desegregation, presumably standing at the viewer's vantage point. The wall behind her reveals their racial slurs and thrown tomatoes. It is 1960.

That painting was based on real events. That little girl, Ruby Bridges, is a real person. She is alive and well as of the writing of this book, younger than Oprah Winfrey, John Travolta, Jerry Seinfeld, Howard Stern, Meryl Streep, Richard Gere, Kathie Lee Gifford, and Tim Gunn. That picture, those opponents, that desegregation battle: none of it was so long ago.

The Long-Time-Ago Illusion

As I write this, I am sitting a few miles from the home of my friend and role model Ina McNeil, a great-great-granddaughter of Chief Sitting Bull, the legendary leader of the Sioux tribes defending their land. As a child, she (along with her siblings and thousands of other children) was taken involuntarily from her parents and required to attend an Indian boarding school operated by the federal Bureau of Indian Affairs. Until Ina told me about these schools a few years ago, and I did my own follow-up reading, I had not heard of them. This is embarrassing. I probably pretended I knew what she was describing at the time and then googled it afterward. Her childhood was not a long time ago, but many of us do not know about this widespread occurrence.

In 1997, Ina shared her story with a reporter: "I remember one time a girl passing a slice of bread over from one table to another in the dining hall." This prompted the ex-military matron, who "came over and grabbed the girl who passed the bread by the hair, lifted her off the chair and threw her on the floor. I was probably in the fifth grade."[1] These traumatic memories remain vivid. She is now eighty years old: vibrant, sharp, and active. None of this was a long time ago. These are people in our communities, in our country, people you and I know.

Here is another example of how history was not long ago. During the pandemic, some people in black communities distrusted the vaccine, fearing medical racism. An oft-cited concern was the now-infamous Tuskegee Experiment, initiated in 1932 by the U.S. Public Health Service and the Centers for Disease Control and Prevention (yes, that CDC). Six hundred impoverished sharecroppers in Alabama signed up for this study in exchange for free medical care. For many, this would be their first time being treated by a doctor, and as sons, husbands, brothers, and fathers, they were pleased at the opportunity. Instead, the government researchers deceived them, withholding treatment and critical health information. As a result, many of the men infected their partners and their children, who suffered from untreated syphilis, resulting in possible blindness, deafness, heart disease, bone deterioration, and death. The study ended in 1972, not because the government or researchers had a change of heart, but because of leaked documents from a whistle-blower.

At the time, Don McLean's "American Pie" and Elton John's "Rocket Man"—two songs that still get lots of airplay—topped our *Billboard* charts. I was on the verge of entering kindergarten, where I would be taught that the civil rights movement had been a success. Yet the Tuskegee Experiment was still happening. Today the surviving children of the study participants are still alive. No doubt, the COVID-19 vaccine and the syphilis studies are not the same thing; everyone who can get the COVID-19 vaccine should. But for those who worry about Tuskegee, it is not a fair critique or persuasive argument to claim that this event was too long ago to be relevant. It's not ancient history.

Our challenge is to overcome what I call the Long-Time-Ago Illusion, as it limits our capacity to engage with the present by connecting dots to the past. We began by examining how little time, and how few generations, stand between historical events and the present. Next we will look at how our knowledge of what happened in the past shapes our perceptions of what is happening in the present. Then we will look at how the past and the present connect through subtle ways, like thought and speech patterns. Finally we will examine the psychology of time and how it further blurs our sense of historical events. Again, we are interrogating the idea that "history" was "a long time ago" to help us see that the past informs the present more than we often realize. Facing our whitewashed past requires us to see and connect those dots. The 1619 Project helps us do this.

The 1619 Project

The 1619 Project began as the brainchild of *New York Times* journalist Nikole Hannah-Jones. In 1619, kidnapped and enslaved Africans were first brought to our shores. To mark the four hundredth year, Hannah-Jones sought to correct the celebratory whitewashed histories that did not accurately place racism and slavery in our past, and in which the residue of these institutions did not live in our present. The initiative essentially countered the Long-Time-Ago Illusion, producing evidence that our understanding of history was inaccurate, and that the implications of those events and our misunderstanding were all around us today.

Hannah-Jones pitched the idea to the *Times* editors and led a monumental undertaking involving dozens of writers who produced a special issue of the *New York Times Magazine,* a podcast, a newspaper section, a children's curriculum, a multitude of stories that appeared throughout the newspaper, and eventually a bestselling book by the same name.[2] When the special issue was published, the *Times* printed hundreds of thousands of extra copies and yet it was still difficult to find a newsstand that was not sold out. The Times Store sold out three times in the first two days after it went on sale. At the *Times* headquarters in New York City, a line stretched down the block near Times Square as two thousand free copies were given away.[3]

Hannah-Jones won the 2020 Pulitzer Prize for Commentary for the 1619 Project. Some letters to the editor noted that the project was a "magnificent gift to our nation," "the very best of journalism's public service," and "the most important piece of journalism I have ever had both the pleasure and pain of reading."[4] Many universities sought to recruit Hannah-Jones, including the University of North Carolina, which offered her a prestigious professorship earmarked for elite journalists.

The 1619 Project has also been controversial. Some critics have taken issue with specific claims, while others feel the overall endeavor is misguided and unpatriotic. In fact, UNC withheld the customary offer of tenure with the job offer, caving to a board resistant to reckoning with our whitewashed past. The university reversed its position only after faculty, students, alumni, and the general public expressed outrage (Hannah-Jones declined the offer and accepted a position at Howard University).

Despite all the noise, the *Times* has felt it necessary to issue only one correction to the work. A correction is no small matter for any serious media outlet, but the fact that there has been only one is extraordinary, given the scope of the provocative argument and the vehemence of the critics. History will always be debated and arguments will be refined, for all the reasons covered in earlier chapters. The 1619 Project is no exception.

After all, the 1619 Project excavates American life so that we can see its roots, and the roots are surprising in multiple ways. First, the roots stretch earlier than our independence from England in 1776. Second, the roots are coated in the blood of enslaved people. Third, those roots have grown into our national foliage in a way that obscures the roots, but nonetheless is their outgrowth.

Hannah-Jones writes, "Out of slavery—and the anti-black racism it required—grew nearly everything that has truly made America exceptional: its economic might, its industrial power, its electoral system, diet and popular music, the inequities of its public health and education, its astonishing penchant for violence, its income inequality, the example it sets for the world as a land of freedom and equality, its slang, its legal system and the endemic racial fears and hatreds that continue to plague it to this day."[5] The 1619 Project explores every item in this list in detail, placing the consequences of slavery and the contributions of black Americans at the center of the story, rather than at the margins or out of the frame entirely.

I found this new lens startling in its starkness, mesmerizing in its meaning, and illuminating in its illustration of connecting the dots between past and present. When we note the disparities plaguing our society today, it makes far more sense that the past would influence the present, than to say that some magical force or self-defeating sabotage is creating these disparities. The Long-Time-Ago Illusion obscured this logical and simple explanation. Once that illusion was shattered, I felt a weird sense of comfort. Things made more sense. There was a cause for the effect. Not understanding our history had made it impossible for me to understand the world I live in now. Apparently I am not alone.

The Marley Hypothesis

The Long-Time-Ago Illusion makes it difficult to see what is in front of us, and how it got there. In particular, the illusion makes it difficult to see systems. When we notice something that seems wrong, such as an all-white neighborhood in a diverse region or a Native American mascot of a sports team, we see an individual incident or the product of individual decisions. We are less likely to see the systems that led to the whiteness of the neighborhood or the mascot choice. Making these systems more visible is a powerful and needed tool.

Singer and songwriter Bob Marley is going to help us in surprising ways, but first, a pop quiz.

True or False?

1. The FBI employed illegal techniques (for example, hidden microphones in motels) in an attempt to discredit African-American political leaders during the civil rights movement.
2. African-American Paul Ferguson was shot outside his Alabama home for trying to integrate professional football.

These questions appeared in a "Black history quiz" written by psychologists Jessica Nelson, Glenn Adams, and Phia Salter.[6] Participants answered each question as true or false, along with a rating of how certain they were of their responses. Their quiz score indicated the participants' knowledge of the past. (For the record, question 1 is true and question 2 is made up. I scored 50 percent.) Then the participants were given incidents from the present and asked to rate the extent to which they were examples of racism.

Black participants were more accurate than white participants at the racism detection task, particularly when it came to detecting systemic racism. The reason, however, was surprising. Their ability to detect racism in the present was a function of their better performance on the history quiz, on which black participants performed three times better than white participants. In other words, participants with better scores on the history quiz were also more likely to detect racism (particularly systemic racism) in the present. The ability to distinguish how racism is perpetuated in systems, not just individuals, is key to performing well in this task. The perception gap (about the present) appeared to be at least partially a knowledge gap (about the past).

The researchers called their discovery the Marley Hypothesis, after legendary reggae musician Bob Marley. In his iconic 1983 song, "Buffalo Soldier," he wails that those who know their history know where they are coming from and thus don't have to ask who they are.[7] Specifically, he sings, "when I analyze the stench, to me it makes a lot of sense." That is the core of the Marley Hypothesis: ignorance of racism in the past leads to denial of racism in the present. This finding clashes with the narrative that black people are "playing the race card" when they see racism where others do not. The issue is not race, but knowledge.

In subsequent work, Salter and coauthors asked nearly four hundred white adults to listen to an approximately ten-minute radio segment from the NPR show *Fresh Air*.[8] Half of the participants learned about historian Richard Rothstein's research over the past two decades into the role of government housing policy in creating black ghettos in the United States; the other half (the control group) learned about research on pig intelligence. Both clips were rated as equally engaging.

Again, the researchers were interested in whether historical knowledge affected how the study participants perceived racism in the present. They found that the racism perception gap narrowed in the history condition but not in the control condition. Again, the Marley Hypothesis shows us what is needed to connect the dots between history and current events, what happened a long time ago and what is happening now.

It is also important to note the nature of the historical knowledge in the experiments that led to the Marley Hypothesis. In earlier chapters, we discussed how people crave and care about knowledge about the past . . . when it is their intimate past. That kind of history evokes nostalgia and collective pride. The kind of history in the earlier true/false questions is likely less craved by white Americans and thereby less familiar. While we are drawn to a particular view of our past, we may need to be drawn to a fuller account of our past. When we have that knowledge, even a very small amount, the payoff is profound. We can better see the world through a perspective different than our own.

The value of this insight is even greater to those who least want to hear it. The more closely white people identified with their group, the less likely they were to have knowledge of the past and to see racism in the present. Also, the more that white people identified with their group, the less impactful it was to build their knowledge of the past. It is as if learning about what happened a long time ago lights up the present, making racism visible to those who might not see it otherwise, but with sunglasses still obscuring the view. While context likely matters in the strength of this effect, seeing the past is related to seeing the present.

Next we explore how the past spills into the present. We begin by focusing on two human activities that are so automatic and fluid that we often ignore their power: thinking and speaking.

Thoughts Get Passed On

To study how past actions might connect to present attitudes, psychologist Keith Payne and colleagues selected the 1860 census as their starting point.[9] That census documented the enslaved proportion of each county's population and its data was embedded in the map President Abraham Lincoln used at the dawn of the Civil War to forecast which states would be most likely to secede.

Payne and colleagues mapped this very old data onto very new data, collected via the web-based Implicit Association Test (IAT). As millions of us now know, because we have taken this free, anonymous test online, the IAT measures implicit biases using response time technology. The test taker groups similar words and images together as quickly as possible, revealing the unconscious cognitive maps of their mind.[10] Based on 25.8 million IATs taken on the public website, 85 percent of white Americans show an implicit race bias in which they have positive associations with white people and negative associations with black people.[11] Many, if not most, of these people do not show an explicit (that is, self-reported and consciously held) bias that matches this implicit bias.

Using IAT data from 2.5 million Americans across the country, Payne and colleagues conducted granular analyses at the state and county levels. They theorized that areas once dependent on enslaved people's labor would have laws, norms, and institutions that supported the enslavement of black people. This social, legal, and economic context would reinforce negative mental associations with black people, both reflecting and justifying the context. Thought of this way, implicit biases can be viewed not only as an individual measure of any particular test taker in a particular context, but also as an aggregate measure of structural and systemic racism in a particular context.

The data revealed that white people living now in counties and states with a higher proportion of their population enslaved in 1860 had greater anti-black implicit bias. The researchers considered the alternative hypothesis that the effect might be a function of the proportion of black residents in the community today, rather than the proportion of enslaved people more than 150 years ago. They found that the implicit biases of white test takers today were uniquely associated with enslaved populations in the past but not with contemporary black populations, and that the implicit biases of black test takers today were the reverse.

Thoughts are passed on from generation to generation. Thoughts are built into how life is lived and society is structured. Structural inequalities, such as economic, cultural, or legal patterns that were seeded during slavery and continue into modern day, feed directly into racial disparities in mobility and poverty. Here we see the connecting of seemingly unrelated dots. Slavery was a long time ago. None of us alive today were alive then. Still, these whitewashed dots are connected.

Speech Carries Attitudes

Birds can fly across oceans and dogs can smell a treat locked in the car, but humans have their own awe-inspiring superpower—speech. On average, humans can construct speech by producing 150 words per minute with minimal effort.[12] And these words are just a fraction of the thoughts we process within that same time frame.

The fluency and automaticity with which our words flow makes language a veritable thumbprint of our minds, just as psychologist Mahzarin Banaji often refers to implicit biases as the thumbprint of culture.[13] This fluency makes speech both hard to change and essential to examine. It is unclear whether our biases—implicit and explicit—are shaping our speech and/or our speech is shaping our biases. Both are probably true.

To understand this better, we can examine patterns in word usage. Scientists at Stanford University have developed sophisticated methods for tracking these patterns via machine-learning analyses of more than 130 billion words from news articles and books from the last century.[14] They looked at the frequency at which words appeared and which were paired more or less frequently with other words.

For example, they found that in 1910, the most common adjectives associated with distinctly Asian (versus white) last names included *barbaric, aggressive, monstrous, hateful, cruel,* and *bizarre.* There was little Asian immigration at this time and Asians were viewed as distant foreigners. In 1950 (not long after World War II), the adjectives included *unstable, venomous, disobedient, predatory,* and *boisterous.* Stereotypes of Asians as traitorous were common at this time. As Asian immigration to the United States increased dramatically after the Immigration and Nationality Act of 1965, we see the overt negativity of the words subside and a new stereotype of the quiet Asian immigrant emerge. In 1990, the words included *passive, haughty, complacent, sensitive,* and *hearty.* These patterns reveal a rich map of society, including stereotypes and demographic shifts.

In another study using a related methodology, a team of artificial intelligence scholars theorized that language carries imprints of our biases.[15] To test their theory, the researchers did a large-scale crawl of the web, gathering everything from celebrity tweets to sports blogs to congressional hearings. The end result was 840 billion total words, comprising about 2.2 million unique words.

Armed with this mass of words, the researchers summoned artificial intelligence and machine learning to create new clusters of words—to learn to "write." In other words, the machines studied human language and then produced humanlike language. The scientists wanted to see what words the AI would associate together.

The researchers then compared the AI word clusters to the results of millions of IAT tests to explore how the patterns of implicit bias compare to the patterns of language in everyday use. They used the findings of the most widely taken IATs—including the race IAT, the gender IAT, and the age IAT—and then tested for those similar stereotypes linguistically. Bear in mind that the Implicit Association Test uses the word association method to measure implicit bias.

Every pattern seen in the implicit bias findings showed up in the language "written" by the computers. The computers mimicked our thoughts. The machine-produced language included word associations such as African-American names with unpleasant words and male names (not female names) with career, math, and science words. In other words, if an alien were to only have access to all of our printed words, they could re-create the cognitive maps of our minds, and vice versa. Together, studies like these quantify how the language we use both reveals and molds our thoughts.

How we speak to and about each other also defines our interactions with each other. It is because language is so important in our relationships that it is so robust and central to our daily lives. Why else would we have more than a million English words plus millions more in other languages to choose from? The richness of our humanity and relationships is captured in the richness of our language . . . both for good and for bad.

These studies illustrate how the past and present are linked through the thought and speech patterns that define human interactions, thread from generation to generation, and weave together the past and the present.

Systems Replicate

Many of our systems today reflect choices of yesterday. For example, housing policy expert Richard Rothstein's book *The Color of Law* delineates how law and policy decisions at the local, state, and federal levels impact how our neighborhoods and communities look today.[16] While individual racism and personal preferences certainly played a role, Rothstein argues that residential segregation today results from direct government actions, including racially separate public housing in cities, exclusionary zoning laws in suburbs, discriminatory neighborhood association rules and restrictive covenants, and tax-exempt status for churches, universities, and hospitals with discriminatory restrictive covenants.

A primary source of equity and wealth in the United States is the rising value of one's home. This appreciating asset then allows for intergenerational wealth transfer, which allows for the next generation to own a home, and so on. Of course, this assumes one owns one's home to begin with. Rothstein delineates the massive legalized barriers to home ownership for black families, as recently as in my childhood in the 1960s and 1970s. Changing those laws does not undo the lack of accumulated wealth and lack of wealth transfer of the past. The systems thus replicate with or without the laws.

Even with new laws and policies, the preexisting impact of the old laws has not been addressed. Thus the patterns and systems continue indefinitely, with or without the original laws that led to the patterns and systems. It is like putting in a new trash bag on top of the already-filled one, instead of taking out the trash.

Ancestors Stay with Us

When Sidney Norman* was nine years old, she learned that her grandmother and her friends had not always lived in Chicago. Like many black people, they had migrated north from the Deep South during the Great Migration. Sidney wanted to know and pursue their stories. With no adult prompting, Sidney found a tape recorder and interviewed her grandmother and her grandmother's friends.

As a young adult, she wrote a book capturing her family's stories and

---

*The name has been changed upon request to protect privacy.

self-published it so that she could give copies to her relatives. She even sought out the descendants of her white great-grandfather, curious to hear their perspective about the secret black family and fifteen-year relationship he had with her great-grandmother "on the side." As a graduate student, she worked as a Harriet Tubman reenactor while writing her thesis from a desk on the site of a former plantation where Tubman hid enslaved people. Clearly, Sidney sees and feels a connection between her ancestors' past and her present.

Today Sidney keeps an ancestor altar in her home. When we spoke by phone, she described the items on the altar with care, sending me pictures afterward. Her maternal great-grandmother carried this coin purse. Her maternal grandmother made and carried this handkerchief, manufactured at the sweatshop factory where she worked. Her paternal grandfather and many men of his generation used this leather strop to sharpen their razors. A bedside bell her grandfather used to summon help when bedridden, a pack of her grandfather's favorite cigarettes, discharge papers from World War II, her great-grandfather's will that included one hundred acres of land purchased soon after emancipation—each item carries the memory and spirit of her ancestors, filled with health and well-being, joy and resilience, blessings and burdens. When she touches these items, she tells me, she knows they were once in the hands of her ancestors.

Now in her thirties, Sidney explains, "There's usually one person in every generation who gets the torch. It's whoever in your family does the family tree and organizes the family reunion. I am that person from my family."

Her role is more than documentation. She does rituals for the dead, provides comfort to dying people, and plans to become a death doula. Sidney has relationships with every branch of her family tree, even the highest, oldest branches of generations no longer alive. These are spiritual relationships in which she interacts with her ancestors. She notes that most religions have similar practices for honoring the dead and connecting with ancestors.

Her voice is clear and steady as she explains, "I can viscerally feel the pain of slavery and of my grandfather's father being lynched. I can go further back in time, energetically and spiritually, for support and strength. I can literally feel the well-being and blessings of my lineage in our ancestral line from before 1619." Her ancestral practices tie her back to Africa and the "wholeness that is in all of us."

She recalls an old spirit "like an Islamic scholar"—not someone she knew specifically but who she felt was from her maternal line dating back to Timbuktu—who would sit with her as she wrote her dissertation. Her writing ritual began by lighting candles, ringing a bell, and saying a little prayer. Then, she remembers, "Each day, he would sit right next to me. He stayed until I finished, and then he was gone."

Debating how much more to disclose to me, she hesitates. She has a high-status job and a prestigious resume that gives her legitimacy in the eyes of some people. She knows some of these people will roll their eyes at her spiritual journey. On the other hand, she is often approached by people—many with resumes as enviable as hers—seeking her help in "spirit work." In her experiences and beliefs, she is far from alone.

As Sidney notes, many traditions—religious, indigenous, spiritual— connect the dots between the past and present via our relationships with our ancestors. In everyday conversation, we speak of traits, beliefs, and affinities that run in the family, are in our blood, don't fall far from the tree, and are handed down through generations; we know we will see our loved ones on the other side, over the rainbow bridge, and when we meet again. Our connections to our ancestors—whatever you believe them to be—make their lives seem not so long ago. And, of course, they also live on in our genetics.

Trauma Persists

In his book *She Has Her Mother's Laugh: The Powers, Perversions, and Potential of Heredity,* science journalist Carl Zimmer tackles complicated questions about lineage.[17] He examines the newest research and oldest assumptions to argue that the way we pass things on to future generations is far more robust than we might have understood. For example, epigenetic researchers have found that we can inherit trauma from our parents, grandparents, and ancestors. Once controversial, the scientific basis for this work has become stronger.

We typically think of trauma as a scar. If I bear a scar on my arm from an accident, my children will not be born with that scar. If I carry my arm a bit differently as a result, it is possible that my children might mimic my body language, thus "inheriting" something from my accident. But my children will not inherit the scar itself.

However, recent research shows that trauma can be passed on in more fundamental ways. Environmental stresses such as trauma can turn our genes on and off without any actual alterations to the genes. Moreover, these alterations, while reversible, can be passed on to future generations. In *The Atlantic*, Nathaniel Comfort wrote, "They are hitchhikers on the chromosomes, riding along for a while, but able to hop on and off."[18]

High school biology class proves relevant here, as we distinguish between genotype (think genes—invisible) and phenotype (think features—visible like hair color). We can't see people's genes; we can see people's features. Epigenetic theories of intergenerational trauma posit that the damage of trauma can pass down through generations through a mechanism that does not affect our genotypes but does affect our phenotypes.

In other words, a narrow genetic explanation of how we inherit things from our ancestors revolves around our DNA. A broader epigenetic explanation of inheritance says that the expression of our DNA is altered by our parents' experiences even if our actual DNA is unchanged.

For example, mice were exposed to a cherry blossom scent while simultaneously receiving a mild shock on the foot, enough to make them fearful.[19] The mice came to associate the scent with the shock. After the male mice bred, they were not allowed to interact with their offspring. Nonetheless, their offspring—and even their offspring's offspring— showed a sensitivity to the cherry blossom scent, as compared to mice in the control condition. They were jumpy and fearful. Scientists found chemical markers on their DNA affecting olfactory functioning, and more neurons in their brains tied to detecting the scent.

Similarly, imagine that a man experiences war, famine, or slavery. In the epigenetic theory, if the trauma occurs before he helps conceive a child, he may pass on the damage to his children in some form. His experience will affect his sperm and, thus, the children born from that sperm. The effects are not driven by his parenting, because the effects are not seen in children conceived before the trauma, only after. A biological marker of the trauma is passed on.

As we think about how to connect the dots of the past to the dots of the present, we must consider how traumatic experiences and their aftermath may be passed on from generation to generation in ways that we are only beginning to understand. Sidney's spiritual lens also detects this intergenerational trauma. "It comes through lineages. If you have enough blessings, intergenerational trauma won't affect you that much. If you have less of those blessings, you can get stuck in those patterns." Whether through genetics, epigenetics, or spirits, the past connects to the present.

We have challenged the Long-Time-Ago Illusion with several examples of how the past connects to the present—through our thoughts, speech, systems, ancestors, and trauma. When we reckon with our whitewashed past, these connections become more visible. Next we explore the psychology of time that can lead us to feel like things are a long-time-ago, even when they are not.

Things Look Blurry Far Away

We begin with the notion of distance. When we look down the street at people, things, or places, we automatically perceive their distance. The car driving in front of us is close. The stop sign at the end of the block is farther. The sun setting on the horizon is farthest. Things that are farther away are blurrier.

Just as our eyes use physical distance to process our external reality, our minds use psychological distance to process our internal thoughts. Subconsciously, we build cognitive maps of our thoughts, much as a physical map orients us to the external world.

Psychologists Yaacov Trope and Nira Liberman have shown that when we think about people, places, and events, we situate them a certain psychological distance from us using four criteria.[20] The closer they are to a) like me, b) here, c) now, and d) reality, the shorter the psychological distance. For example, if I am thinking of another (real) female professor (me) in New York City (here) this week (now), that will be a low psychological distance thought. In contrast, when I think of a fictional (not real) male Jedi guide (not me) a long time ago (not now) in a galaxy far, far away (not here), this thought is more likely to evoke high psychological distance.

We process thoughts differently based on their psychological distance. When psychological distance is short, we tend to think in concrete terms, whereas when it is far, we think in abstract terms. If I am thinking about my meeting this afternoon, I will think about the meeting's time and location: concrete thoughts. If I am thinking about my meeting scheduled for next month, I will think more about the purpose of the meeting: abstract thoughts. Again, details blur with greater distance.

Understanding psychological distance is useful to appreciating the challenges of connecting the dots between the past and present. If I learn about a kidnapping that happened last week (versus one a century ago) or to someone like me (versus someone not like me) or ten miles from me (versus ten thousand miles from me), I will engage with this information in more vivid and concrete terms. The farther the psychological distance, the less real it will feel to me.

Psychological distance also shapes how we place blame. Psychologists have also found that we put more blame on victims from a long time ago (psychologically far) than on victims from more recent events (psychologically close).[21] Further, we tend to ascribe a "silver lining" narrative to the long-ago victim, expecting they will have incurred benefits from their suffering.

We also tend to feel less emotional intensity for psychologically distant events than for psychologically close events.[22] If we hear there was a terrible fire this morning, as opposed to ten years ago or a hundred years ago, we will likely have a stronger emotional response to the more recent fire. Similarly, horrified as we are at the absurd idea of segregated water fountains in the last century, we would be even more horrified at the thought of it happening today.

Consider this tragic example: Carolyn Bryant, whose false accusations of fourteen-year-old Emmett Till in 1955 led a racist mob to lynch him, is still alive. But I suspect our emotional response toward her horrific "Karen" actions more than six decades ago are not as strong as those we might have toward someone taking the same actions yesterday. Effectively, our minds blur the past and mute our emotions. This tendency feels like a close cousin of the hindsight bias we have discussed in earlier chapters; the bad thing a long time ago takes on an inevitable quality.

To recap, as psychological distance grows—as it does with events long ago about people different from us—our tendency to blur the specifics and blame the victims also grows. So while the past may not actually be that long ago, it tends to feel blurry and distant. Psychological distance makes it easy to assume the past was a long time ago and hard to connect the dots between then and now.

Wrinkles in Time

If you say TGIF to colleagues at work on Friday, you're communicating more than words. When we look forward to something in the future, we "pre-experience" it. Our lateral prefrontal[23] cortex and frontopolar cortex see increased activity because we experience anticipatory emotion.[24] Looking forward to that upcoming weekend barbecue is part of the pleasure we get from the barbecue. We even perceive a barbecue tomorrow as being closer in time than a barbecue yesterday because we perceive temporal distance the same way we perceive spatial distance.

That is, just as our bodies move in a particular direction in physical space, we perceive ourselves moving in a particular direction in temporal space. This makes the future seem closer than the past.

Researchers find that pre-experiencing an event feels different than recalling an event. We experience more intense emotion when anticipating the barbecue than we do when remembering the barbecue afterward.[25] This asymmetry between our past and future emotional experiences starts young. Even six-year-olds show these asymmetric effects when looking forward to a holiday versus reflecting on it.

The bottom line: our minds process events in the future differently than events in the past. Psychologist Eugene Caruso and his colleagues call this phenomenon a "wrinkle in time."[26] This psychological wrinkle has important implications for our moral judgments. In theory, a morally questionable behavior that happened yesterday and the same behavior happening tomorrow should feel equivalently problematic. However, just as we experience more intense emotions about tomorrow's barbecue versus yesterday's one, we also experience more intense moral judgments about tomorrow's ethical lapse than we do about yesterday's. In one study, management's broken promise to union workers was judged more harshly one week before it happened than one week after. In another wrinkle-in-time study, a mock jury awarded more to an accident victim for pain and suffering that was described as being in the future versus in the past.

Because the "future looms larger" than the past morally, people also feel more collective guilt for a future transgression than a past one and are even willing to offer more compensation for what will happen versus what has happened.[27] This counterintuitive tendency becomes even more worrisome when combined with our tendency to believe that people tend to get what they deserve, known as a just world belief.[28] Harm that takes place farther back in time is more likely to lead to a blaming of the victim, versus more recent harm.

Our muted moral and emotional response to the past has important implications for facing our whitewashed past. We will be less appalled by historical atrocities. This more forgiving psychology leaves us in an awkward position when evaluating the impact that the past has had on the present. Our responses are even more muted as we talk about a past that we perceive as being a long time ago.

Four Ways to Connect the Dots

In summary, the less we know about the past, the less we will understand its impact on the present. Yet we are psychologically wired to downplay the past and overplay the future. To counter these tendencies, we want to connect the dots. Here are four tips for doing that.

First, see the seduction of nostalgia. As Billy Joel sings, "The good ol' days weren't always good." This truth does not mean that there is not any good in the past; only that no time in the past was all good for all people. When we are offered a gauzy gaze at the past, we should ask who did not benefit from those good times.

Second, think critically about disparities. It is human nature to normalize what we encounter frequently. We adapt to and accept much of our surroundings, without questioning their origins or investigating what in the past led to the present. For example, if black people and white people live in different neighborhoods today, we can ask why. The key to reckoning is to notice and interrogate disparities, rather than normalizing and accepting them.

Third, seek different perspectives on the same event. Every family has a story where no one can agree on what really happened. The same phenomenon happens at a societal level. Assemble the puzzle pieces of history by hearing not just the view of the victorious or powerful, but also the views of the defeated, enslaved, or powerless. Ask whose voices are missing.

Fourth, wonder about the backstory. There is always a tale about how a company got its name, how a family adopted a tradition, or how a town declared a holiday. Dig into those stories. Why is it named that? Why is it placed there? Why do we celebrate that? Consider how that choice in the past aligns with our aspirations for the present.

Millions of people alive today have cells, nightmares, memories, and scars that date back to "historical" events. Events of our history books haunt their dreams and daily lives. In the United States, every complete generation (a generation that has made it through its average life expectancy of roughly eighty years) has lived under race-defined laws. Every single one. These events were not a long time ago. Their impact is still with us.

When we reckon with the past, we will connect the dots like the hands of multiple generations descended from an enslaved person, pulling the rope of an old bell. As we see how the past lives in the present, we will start to question the stories we have long believed to be true. In the next chapter, we focus on how to detect and reject the fables.

Reject Racial Fables

Where I'm from, we believe all
sorts of things that aren't true.
—*WICKED*

A Day in the Life of Activist Louise McCauley

In the winter of 1955, a forty-two-year-old African-American activist named Louise McCauley left work after a busy day juggling her job responsibilities with the activism that consumed her off hours. Always energetic, she had spent her coffee break on the phone with a college president speaking about an NAACP workshop she was planning on his campus to generate more student activism during this demoralizing time of Jim Crow.

McCauley played a leadership role in the NAACP. She had first attended meetings in the 1930s and was elected to serve on a three-person executive committee of the NAACP state conference in the 1940s. Her wide-ranging activities included writing letters to Congress in favor of antilynching laws and interviewing black people who had been attacked by white people to document the incidents, even if disregarded by law enforcement. Community organizing and activism work was a huge part of her life.

Young McCauley had been known for her defiance of Jim Crow norms and laws. A childhood friend recalls that "nobody ever bossed her around and got away with it." In fact, McCauley's grandmother, who had been enslaved, openly feared her granddaughter would be lynched before she was twenty years old. The family moved in with family members in a different neighborhood to avoid scenarios where Louise would encounter taunting white kids on the way to school. Louise McCauley did not seek fights but she also did not avoid them, and that could lead to trouble for her more than the protected white kids.

At a time when black people were blocked from voting by onerous poll taxes, literacy tests, or needing a white person to vouch for them, McCauley kept trying to register to vote even after being rejected multiple times. Once, she noticed that the registrar seemed open to sharing the answers to the registration test with two white women in line, while denying Louise's application. On her third try, she hand-copied all of the questions so she could prove that she had passed, and if needed, bring suit against the voter registration board. She eventually joined the 3 percent of eligible black people in the South who were registered to vote and was active in helping others do the same. She did not accept that norms, rules, or laws were fair just because they existed, and was tenacious in her efforts.

McCauley knew the odds were against her. The efforts of her and her fellow activists had not yielded the visible progress they had hoped for in the past. She said, "It was hard to keep going when all our efforts seemed in vain." Nevertheless, McCauley had a track record as a relentless, longtime fighter of the status quo.

Among other things, she and the other volunteers were planning an act of civil disobedience. When the time came, they planned that McCauley would defy legal statutes and cultural norms that mandated that a black person of any age or sex had to stand up and yield their seat to any white person. That Thursday, on her way home from that busy day at work, turned out to be the day. McCauley was well suited for the challenging, potentially fatal, act of civil disobedience that awaited her that day after work.

McCauley was told to yield her spot by the white man in charge, who carried a gun. This was not her first run-in with him, and she recalled that in the first incident, she had told him, "You better not hit me."

"Are you going to stand up?" he demanded. She held her ground.

The police arrived and asked why she was not standing up. She asked the officer, "Why do you all push us around?" She was arrested.

It was not the first time someone had tried this, but something about this incident made it go 1950s viral. Word spread. People mobilized. Dr. Martin Luther King Jr. joined the effort.

And that is how the legendary Montgomery Bus Boycott was born. Activist Louise McCauley—whose full name was Rosa Louise McCauley Parks—would not give up her seat on the bus.

The Story We Tell

When I first heard the truth about Rosa Parks, I was hit by a one-two punch of surprise and embarrassment. First, I was surprised, like when I found out the identity of Luke Skywalker's father. Mind blown. Second, I was embarrassed. Rosa Parks has the second most recognizable historical name in America (outside of presidents and first ladies).[1] How could I be ignorant of such basic facts about her?

Alas, I am not alone. After all, you and I have heard the story a million times: Rosa Parks was an elderly black seamstress on her way home from work who stayed seated in the whites-only section of a segregated bus in Montgomery, Alabama, because her feet were tired. We learned that her spur-of-the-moment act sparked the Montgomery Bus Boycott and the civil rights movement, giving this usually docile woman an accidental place in history.

While the fable has never been true, it was what we all learned. By the time of the 1955 bus incident, Parks described herself as having "a life history of being rebellious." The evidence is well documented and supports her account. She tried to correct our national narrative. "I was not tired physically, or no more tired than I usually was at the end of a working day. . . . No, the only tired I was, was tired of giving in." Rosa Parks was tireless. Nevertheless, the fable—and our national ignorance—persisted.

It was not until 2013 that the first full-length, footnoted, serious biography written by a historian and intended for adults told the real story. In *The Rebellious Life of Mrs. Rosa Parks* (also available in a young adult version and now as a film), award-winning historian Jeanne Theoharis challenged what she called the "national fable."[2] The book was published fifty-eight years after the bus incident and eight years after Parks died. The primary documents were clear about the true history and the facts were not buried, scandalous, or secret. Still, they were not well known. Rosa Parks has one of the most recognized names in the United States and yet one of the least recognized stories.

The fable, Theoharis writes, is "a powerful story of individual grit and American courage, filled with good guys and bad guys and a happy ending." The harder story, says Theoharis, is both "more beautiful and more terrible" than the familiar ones. "Most people don't do the right thing [and yet] it is breathtaking to see what people did to build these movements. It's more inspiring and more depressing [than what we believe]." Rosa Parks was not the first to try what she tried. Others had before her, with less visible impact. The fable does not capture the paradoxical futility and importance of those earlier attempts. The fable—fueled by the hindsight bias—leads us to take that iconic Rosa Parks moment for granted, rather than appreciating how she and her lifetime of activism were far from inevitable.

What Theoharis observes as a historian syncs up with what psychologists find. Human beings use stories to make sense of the world, and fables are a particularly attractive type of story. It starts when we are babies.

Storytelling Animals

Picture a baby watching a screen on which simple shapes move. A circle, a triangle, and a square float across the monitor, programmed to move randomly. At one point, the circle moves toward the square. As the circle approaches, the square moves away and toward the triangle. Does the baby perceive each shape as independent, floating on its own random path? Or does the baby see a story unfolding, in which the square would rather be close to the triangle than the circle?

According to studies, babies see a story, even when there is none. Using the babies' eye movements, startle reactions, and looking time, psychologists construct the story the baby is telling itself, even when the baby does not have language to communicate it. We seem wired as humans[3] to seek narratives in the world around us.[4] Both our baby and adult minds translate stimuli into simple, fable-like stories.

English professor Jonathan Gottschall calls human beings "storytelling animals." He explains: "For humans, story is like gravity: an inescapable field of force that influences everything, but is so omnipresent that we hardly notice it." Even before babies can speak, they are telling themselves stories about the world.

The problem is that the stories tend to be simple, like those shapes on the screen, while the real world is far more complex. Fables are seductive yet false. They are not the bane of the right or the left; fables populate the minds of both conservatives and liberals.

Our challenge is to spot and reject these fables, lest they misguide us about how to handle complex situations in our present-day lives. Like an outdated map, they lead us down the wrong path and toward dead ends. Those of us who believe the fables will blame the victims and protesters of injustice, rather than the perpetuators and beneficiaries. We will quit too soon in advocating for change because we will expect easy victory rather than halting progress. We will lose the trust of those who see and are affected by racism because we will ignore obvious harm done by our heroes in favor of a flawless narrative. Fables are not only false; they are costly.

Three red flags often characterize fables.

Red Flag #1: Clear Cause and Effect

In fables, it is always clear what causes what. This transparency of cause and effect appeals to our natural tendency to try to make sense of the world, called "spontaneous causal thinking."[5] We see a person running and then hear sirens; we assume the police are pursuing the person. We eat a new food and then feel queasy; we assume the food made us sick. We feel a little off in a meeting and then we are excluded from a group email; we assume that we are being punished. Our minds construct cause-effect relationships, even where no relationship exists. We forget the truth of the cliché, "Correlation is not causation." But we ascribe false causation for a reason: when we know what led to what, we feel better equipped to predict the future and to attach meaning to the past. This predictability is comforting.

Such rigid cause-and-effect thinking lends itself toward events unfolding in a discrete and tight timeframe. When events are proximate in time and space, they appear related, and vice versa. So, even if the motion of a circle, square, and triangle is random, our minds ascribe cause and effect. Similarly, even if what caused the movements happened long before the circle made its move, or if there were multiple causes, our minds cannot grasp this possibility as easily.

We see this kind of simplified thinking in the Rosa Parks fable. In reality, multiple acts of civil disobedience over a long period of time in Montgomery preceded the one that made headlines. Previous actions built the networks, skills, knowledge, strategies, and courage that led to the act that happened to light a fuse. But that story lacks an obvious cause-and-effect, particularly because the previous acts did not produce visible, immediate change. If a cause falls in the forest and does not have an effect, was it a cause? In our "storytelling animal" minds, it was not.

Thus the Rosa Parks fable truncates the longer story of the civil rights movement. The photo is cropped, removing the context and background, and leaving only one focal person and one focal action. Truth is replaced by fable.

Red Flag #2: Flawless Heroes

"Never meet your heroes" is sage counsel when it comes to meeting the photo-edited influencer you follow obsessively on Instagram. You are likely to find a less interesting, less kind, less witty, and less attractive person than the one you have been envisioning. Exceptions only seem to prove the rule.

Perhaps the inverse rule applies to our historical figures. The passage of centuries or decades has effectively Instagrammed our heroes, flattening their complex humanity. In reality, our founding fathers who negotiated the Declaration of Independence and the Constitution wrote bills of rights but they also had bills to pay. They took ethical stances but they also sometimes slid down a slippery slope of ethics. They could be both noble in intention and petty in defense. They seemed polished on paper but some were probably socially awkward at parties. The bold-face names in our history books were literally as human as your next-door neighbor, your partner, or your mail carrier. Yet flawless heroes dominate our fables.

Why are hero narratives so attractive? Psychologists say hero narratives address important human needs. First, these stories reveal what we care about and what we believe. The narrative is a value statement. Second, the stories "promote moral elevation, heal psychic wounds, inspire psychological growth, and exude charisma"; in other words, they help us feel good.[6] That moral elevation elicits awe, a uniquely human emotion, that helps us transcend our "small selves" and see ourselves as part of a vast and larger world.[7] When in awe, we are more likely to be generous, ethical, and prosocial in our behavior.

While awe is powerful, we know how to be in awe of someone without romanticizing them into a flawless hero. Perhaps it is a parent, grandparent, or sibling. Perhaps it is a teacher or coach. There is likely someone in each of our lives whom we admire and whose flaws we can see. We can see the entirety of someone's humanity, and when we don't, that is a red flag.

Our glorification of people such as our founding fathers puts us in a bind. No one today will live up to those standards, unless we also make them heroes in distorting and disturbing ways. Moreover, we increase the psychological difficulty of learning about topics like slavery because we have categorized our founding fathers as flawless heroes, not humans. Heroes who inspire awe exist in real life; flawless heroes only exist in fables. The challenge is how to marry awe-inspiring narratives with factual truth, so that we can see, support, and replicate actual heroism.

Red Flag #3: Good Guys Beat Bad Guys

In fables, the good guys always beat the bad guys. If you lose, it is because you are a bad guy, consistent with the good-guys-win mindset of system justification theory. In the civil rights movement fable, the good guys saw that the bad guys were racist. Most people were good guys who quickly agreed to take a stand. The good guys swiftly solved the problem and high-fived. Because good guys outnumbered bad guys, the outcome was inevitable.

Except that scenario never happened. Most people of the time did not support the civil rights movement. Remember that iconic black-and-white footage of the March on Washington and Dr. Martin Luther King Jr's "I Have a Dream" speech? Three years after that, only 36 percent of white Americans believed that Dr. King was helping the cause of civil rights.[8] Many—most—people believed he was moving too fast. The "good guys" were not in the majority. The outcome was hardly inevitable, as prior attempts in decades past had shown that the good guys did not always win nor were they bad guys because they got beat time after time. Nothing was inevitable, though our hindsight bias might say otherwise.

Looking to the past, after changes have already transpired, we revere the Rosa Parkses and view their change efforts as faits accomplis. Yet, in the present, many of us are critical of people pushing for change. We demonize or "not-the-time-and-place" the Colin Kaepernicks. We justify the system and tone police those challenging it. This asymmetric pattern explains why Muhammad Ali was considered too radical and "the most hated man in America" in the 1960s, yet lit the torch at the Centennial Olympic Games in Atlanta in 1996 to an adoring public.[9] Just because something seemed inevitable does not mean it was inevitable.

When we fail to account for the gravity of system justification, the work of Rosa Parks and others appears far easier than it was at the time. We underestimate the public backlash and overestimate the public backing. Thus the fable creates a system-justifying spiral, in which we continue to resist change in the present and fail to see the pattern from the past.

High Stakes

To recap, human beings like stories. In particular, we are drawn to fables, even though they distort the truth and leave us ill-prepared for reality. That's the bad news, but the good news is that fables often feature three red flags—clear cause-and-effect, flawless heroes, and good guys beating bad guys—that help us spot and reject them in favor of learning the truth.

Learning the truth is more than knowing a few fun facts to pull out for game show trivia. When we buy into the fable, we miscalculate how change happens and our agency in driving that change. We underweigh protests because "they do not accomplish anything." We critique activists whom we see as "snowflakes" who should "get a job." We overweigh the impact of heroes, thus letting ourselves off the hook for doing our part. We expect modern-day heroes to be flawless and we tear down those who are flawed, even as they sacrifice so much on our collective behalf. Ironically, we undermine the changes we intend to support because we keep seeking a fable-like story and characters in our present-day world, when none existed then or exist now. If we get better at rejecting the fables of the past, we can get better at not expecting them in the present.

"Oh!" Moments

As a beginner fable spotter, I convinced myself that the problem was my half-hearted efforts in history classes. In high school and college, the subject was not calling my name and I now feel the effects in my mediocre foundation of historical knowledge. If only I had paid more attention to history earlier, I might not be surprised so often by my fable-ridden knowledge.

Then I spoke to historian Pamela Toler, a lifelong history lover who has written eight books, including the recent *Women Warriors,* and a popular history blog (pamelatoler.com). She strives to translate history in compelling, accessible ways for general audiences. In historical knowledge, Pamela is my opposite—a true expert. When I reached her by phone, Pamela was sitting at her writer's desk in Chicago, her cat at her feet, deep in factual research for her next book. I imagined her study and knowledge base was free of fables.

Pamela laughed at my misconception, telling me that when she digs into the facts, she is "regularly" taken aback by the prevalence of fables in her historical understanding. I am stunned and ask her to elaborate. There are versions of history that we learned when we were young, she explains, that are "absolutely wrong, but emotionally satisfying." She talks about the "comic book history"—aka fables—so many of us learned. She rattles off a few examples, such as the cheery hospitality of Thanksgiving, George Washington chopping down a tree, and Abraham Lincoln writing the Gettysburg Address in just a few minutes on the back of an envelope.

I am astounded that experts like her are prone to believing fables. Pamela is not. "I will never reach the point when I don't have those 'oh!'

moments," she says. "Once you're used to not knowing, you keep stumbling upon things you didn't know. I often find myself saying, 'Oh, here it is again.' The more you know, the more you know." She recalls her research into the mutiny in India . . . and then realized that what was a mutiny to the British was an uprising to the Indians. Every time it happens, she pauses to regroup. "It feels like being slapped upside the head. I stop. I mean, there is literally a stop."

Pamela's vivid metaphor reminds me of the one-two surprise-shame punch, except she dodges the shame jab. Her expertise is not only in historical knowledge, but in the skill of rejecting fables without shame.

The Fable of My Own Life

I am the child of immigrants who left everything and everyone to move to America, the land of opportunity. When my dad was a kid in an Indian village in the state of Punjab, lacking electricity or indoor plumbing, he dreamed of traveling the globe. When my mom was a kid moving between towns in northern India, she dreamed of contact lenses to correct her vision and a pretty music box with a spinning dancer and delicate music. Today my dad has traveled for work or pleasure to more than one hundred countries and my mom not only got contact lenses, she also got LASIK surgery, all the better to see her pretty music box. My parents worked hard—unbelievably hard—and their socioeconomic ascent reflects the so-called American dream.

I grew up understanding that the United States was eager to welcome my parents. People in our Indian-American community often spoke of the shortage of professionals with scientific credentials in America that led to the U.S. government encouraging Indian doctors, engineers, and scientists to immigrate. My dad was a petroleum engineer, so this was their chance. After filling out countless forms and borrowing money, he obtained a visa to the United States; six months later, my mother and I followed. Thanks to the Immigration and Nationality Act of 1965, my family became proud Americans.

We have long been proud not just to enjoy the American dream but to represent the dream of America. More than fifty years later, I realized that my narrative of why we immigrated was based on a fable.

Ironic Plot Twist

The United States had long claimed to be a nation of immigrants.[10] But, in 1960, seven out of eight immigrants came from Europe, which then represented only 20 percent of the world's population. This skew toward white Europeans was not accidental. Many lawmakers explicitly sought to preserve the Judeo-Christian nature of the United States and avoid an influx of brown and black immigrants from countries with developing economies in Asia and Africa. If we were a nation of immigrants, then we were—by design—a nation of white immigrants.

Then came the civil rights movement, including the Civil Rights Act of 1964. This landmark legislation outlawed discrimination based on race, color, religion, sex, national origin, and later, sexual orientation and gender identity. The law had implications for voting, education, housing, employment, and public spaces.

The 1965 immigration law applied the same egalitarianism to immigration. "We have removed all elements of second-class citizenship from our laws by the Civil Rights Act," proclaimed Vice President Hubert Humphrey. "We must in 1965 remove all elements in our immigration law which suggest there are second-class people." President Lyndon Johnson signed the bill at an outdoor ceremony beneath the Statue of Liberty. He described the law as "correct[ing] a cruel and enduring wrong in the conduct of the American nation."

To the dismay of the law's opponents, people from every country now had a path to the American dream. Cosponsored by Democratic senator Philip Hart of Michigan and Democratic representative Emanuel Celler of New York, the law prioritized immigrants with "especially advantageous" skills, like my engineer dad.

However, despite the speechwriters' words and the symbolic formal ceremonies, the decision makers did not actually intend or believe that much would change. In fact, the bill got passed with the assurances that nothing would change. Like so many other artifacts in our history, the words were not intended to be fulfilled, at least not anytime soon. President Johnson reassured opponents that the law was not revolutionary and that the status quo would remain secure. To further placate critics, an added provision shifted priority status away from those with special skills and toward those seeking to join their families in the United States. This provision comforted critics who believed that "chain migration" would ensure that European immigrants remained the prototypical new Americans.

I grew up believing that my country invited us, even recruited us. In fact, there was little widespread support to open American borders to anyone beyond white, European immigrants. American lawmakers underestimated how many Asian and African immigrants would want to come to the United States and how vigorous their efforts to chain-migrate their families would be. Johnson and others were betting that they could claim moral high ground with the new law while retaining America's demographic character.

They lost that bet. By 2010, nine of ten immigrants to the United States came from outside of Europe. Journalist Tom Gjelten of *The Atlantic* summarized this twist as "the irony at the heart of a law whose most revolutionary provision was originally intended to bolster the status quo." The result of that law, egalitarian as it sounded on paper, was never intended by either its proponents or opponents.

My family was among the initial surge. We first arrived in California. My dad got a job as a petroleum engineer at Texaco and my mom got us settled and resettled as we were transferred to a new town (and school for me) in Texas and New Mexico every year until I was nine. Eventually we settled in New Jersey. Throughout my childhood, we were often the only or among the first Indians in the towns in which we lived. I believe I was the only Indian-American in my high school graduating class of about 250 (0.4 percent), and I think, one of three South Asian Americans. Many immigrants would follow. A recent census showed that about half of my hometown is of East or South Asian descent, versus 4.5 percent in 1980, a ten-fold increase.[11] Diwali is even a school holiday. Talk about an ironic plot twist.

Believing In the American Dream

My family came here. We made it. But our American dream was not America's dream. My family is the scenario the law intended to avoid. This law was the polite invitation that you are expected to decline. This law was the empty seat that you did not realize was saved for someone else. This law was the big sale that was sold out before you got there. This law was the "we should get together" you say when you run into someone you don't like. I—and many others—believed the fable.

Most important, many of us failed to realize that we were beneficiaries of the civil rights movement. Without it, we probably would not be here. The same people who opposed the Civil Rights Act of 1964 opposed the Immigration and Nationality Act of 1965. The same people who sat in, stayed seated, marched on, got arrested, and died . . . those same people were fighting for *us*. This is a reality that I do not hear mentioned often in my community.

Many of us did not appreciate that we came here despite white supremacy and because of civil rights advocates. We did not realize that we thrived in a system in which we worked hard, but so did our black brothers and sisters, with less to show for it. Because the system worked for (some of) us, many of us misunderstood it to be working for all of us. We proudly claimed the model minority title. We missed the chance to decolonize our minds. As a result, some of us have perpetuated the meritocracy fable rather than trying to make it a reality.

We have inadvertently reinforced the very forces who opposed our presence in the first place. I wish I had known the truth, not the fable.

Fables Are Everywhere

Our historical knowledge is peppered with fables like Rosa Parks. Thanksgiving. Columbus. Honest Abe. George Washington and the cherry tree. Thomas Jefferson's belief in equality. Once we start looking for fables, we will see them everywhere, waving their red flags.

Here are some fable-spotting questions to ask yourself when hearing a story about an event in the past. Are there any loose ends? If not, then that is a sign that the cause-and-effect relationship is a bit too tidy. Are there heroes who could do no wrong? If so, then that is a sign that the human behind the awe-inspiring hero has been obscured. Do the good guys always win and the bad guys always lose? If yes, then that signals an unlikely world in which the system is always just.

After detecting a fable, the next step is to reject it. To put this in practical terms, think of all the choices available to a Hollywood filmmaker in telling a story. She could shoot the scene from one character's perspective or shoot the same scene multiple ways to see different characters' perspectives. Similarly, when we confront a fable, we need to use our favorite search engine to seek alternate perspectives. Try typing something like "Native American perspective of Thanksgiving" or "surprising facts about Thanksgiving"; terms like *perspective* and *surprising* unlock sources that you might not find otherwise. Naturally, a plethora of misinformation pollutes the internet, but many reliable, well-documented sources are now a click away.

Another filmmaker choice is between a wide shot showing the larger context or a close shot showing only the focal actor. A wide shot would include other things happening at the same time in the background of the fable, such as the removal of Native Americans from their land. Filmmakers also sometimes share what an individual remembers, and then show what actually happened or different individuals' recollections of what happened. Look for oral histories of an event and note similarities and differences among the accounts. To provide background, filmmakers sometimes roll footage of actions that did not lead to any visible impact at the time yet planted seeds for the happenings of the present. This approach is the equivalent of reading "biographies" of issues that cover a longer span of time for a particular issue, allowing more complicated cause-and-effect relationships to surface. These mental filmmaking tools help us reject the fable and set out to reckon with the truer story of this nation we love.

Putting the Tools to Work

In Part A, we discussed How Do We Start, preparing for what is coming. We grabbed two psychological tools: seeing the problem and dressing for the weather. In Part B, we moved to What Do We Do. We examined three psychological tools—embracing the paradoxes of American history, connecting the dots between the past and present, and rejecting fables obscuring facts—that make it possible for us to emotionally and intellectually do the necessary unlearning. The key so far has been to think differently. Next, in Part C, we discuss Where Do We Go from Here, with psychological tools that allow us to have impact in a sustained and resilient way: taking responsibility and building grit.

Part C

Where Do We Go from Here?

Take Responsibility

America is an old house.
We can never declare the work over.
—ISABEL WILKERSON

This Old House

When we own an old house, we expect flaws and imperfections. We don't assume the old house will fix itself, that it is someone else's problem, or that it matters whether the problem began before we moved in. We know that the price of the character, charm, and history includes ownership of the problems. We know that avoiding the problem worsens the problem.

An ignored leak becomes a flooded basement. An untended hairline crack becomes a giant jag. I imagine that people who love these kinds of old houses are prepared, even enthusiastic, about taking care of them. They investigate that leak faster, they seal that crack more carefully. They risk discomfort to check that hard-to-reach corner.

This old-house metaphor comes from Pulitzer Prize winner Isabel Wilkerson in her book *Caste: The Origins of Our Discontents*. Our country is our old house, she says, and we need to investigate what is happening in the basement. Regardless of whether we caused the problem in the basement of our old house, it is our responsibility to fix it.

When it comes to our country, however, we have different expectations and lower tolerance for flaws than we do for old houses. This tendency is the patriot's dilemma we discussed in Chapter 1, in which our love for our country inhibits our willingness to take care of it. When we do not take care of houses, or countries, they deteriorate and decay.

This book is an owner's manual and toolkit for going into the basement. The focus is on how to fix what we find—and not abandon the work midway—by taking responsibility and building grit. We start with Dixie Beer.

Iconic Brands

Jim Birch was on the road visiting a brewery when his cell phone rang. Raised in a white family in New Jersey, he now worked in Charlotte, North Carolina, leveraging his MBA skills in the brewery business. This call was from a headhunter who had some thrilling news. Dixie Beer wanted Jim to run their business.

Founded in 1907, Dixie Beer was an iconic local brand with a loyal following in New Orleans, a beverage that Jim says was "part of every family occasion, or gathering, or sporting event" in the city. The company had survived Prohibition, beer industry consolidation, and Hurricane Katrina, but was now languishing. Production no longer took place in New Orleans. When Jim got that call, the company's new owners planned to invest in the company, the brand, and the city with a new factory, national distribution plan, and general manager. He had a long to-do list and needed to hit the ground running.

Things started out as planned. Jim and his team built a state-of-the-art production facility and did extensive research on how their brand was perceived. They asked people, "What does Dixie mean to you?" and he recalls, "Ninety-nine percent plus told very great stories." It was a strong, nostalgia-soaked, New Orleans–specific brand and people wanted production back in New Orleans. The plan to come back with a stronger Dixie Beer brand was validated and under way.

Things got more nuanced, however, as they moved into their national distribution strategy. Outside of the region, wholesalers were questioning the brand and the meaning of the name Dixie. Jim recalled them asking if Dixie Beer was okay with their name. "And we were just like, 'Yeah, we think we are. Why? What's the issue?'" he recalled. Some people saw an issue, for sure.

He and his colleagues began to wonder. While the actual origins of the word *Dixie* are not fully known, many—including those at Dixie Beer—believe the word stemmed from *dix,* which means "ten" in French. Founded by the French, New Orleans's currency once included the French dix note, which became known as a "dixie." Today *Dixie* is seen by some as a synonym for *southern.*

Still, it became more clear that while it may not have been the intention, Dixie—the word and the brand—evoked a nostalgic view of the Confederacy, Jim Crow, white supremacy, segregation, and slavery. "That became a louder drumbeat in our discussions over several months in the first and second quarter of 2020," he remembers, even as COVID shut them down. Jim acknowledged to me that through this process, he was "still learning about history. I'm surprised by the extent to which institutional racism still exists." He and his team decided to listen and learn.

At the time, Jim says he and his colleagues were grappling internally with the issue. There were no protests about the company's name. No one was "canceled" on social media for drinking the beer. That might have eventually happened, but perhaps because they were already rebooting with a new facility, new distribution approach, and new strategy, they were primed for change and doing the examination themselves. Eighteen months prior, as he surveyed his mountainous to-do list, changing the company's name had not crossed Jim's mind. Now it was on the front burner for the company's owners, board, and general manager.

By the time George Floyd was murdered on May 25, 2020, and the Black Lives Matter movement became higher profile, the company was already actively discussing changing the Dixie name. Because this change had been set in motion earlier in the year, their decision appeared to happen quickly on the heel of the country's "racial reckoning." On June 28, 2020, Dixie Beer announced that it would be retiring its iconic name and selecting a new one. Some cynics wondered if it was a performative corporate response, yet another CEO statement peppered with phrases like "systemic racism" and "doing more." Based on what Jim told me, and to my outsider ear, that critique seemed less applicable to Dixie Beer, especially if one has ever worked in a company, particularly an older one. I suspect the decision was accelerated but not caused by current events. The alternative explanation is that a company with an iconic hundred-year-old brand went from embracing to abandoning that brand in four weeks. It seems implausible.

"Ultimately, it was pretty easy to decide what to do," Jim recalls. Less easy, he says, was the execution. "We had a million cans with a Dixie Beer label sitting in the warehouse to deal with!" Predictably, the decision brought forth some haters, with tweets like "Way to cave to the 8% of people who bitch the loudest" and "Dixie Beer surrenders to the culture jihadists." Jim and his colleagues stood their ground, and eventually started to question whether many of the haters were even their customers or merely trolls.

I Could Not Defend It

The timeline between January 1, 2019 (when Jim accepted a job to revitalize the Dixie Beer brand) to June 28, 2020 (when he became responsible for retiring the name Dixie Beer) was punctuated by moments of learning and surprise. After the public announcement, the surprises continued. Jim was not expecting the gratitude. Many members of the black community told Jim and his colleagues that they appreciated the decision. "The most powerful thing that we heard from some other colleagues and some folks in the African-American community was that 'I was never offended by it, but I never could defend it either.'" Jim had not heard this in the research they had been doing for the previous year and a half. He says this reaction taught him something important.

"When you ask a population that is so homogenous, you're not going to really get the breadth of true feelings that you're looking for," Jim realized, in hindsight. He concluded that many people had always taken issue with the name Dixie and its historical associations; they had just never been asked or listened to. Particularly when it comes to issues like racism, it matters whom you ask and it matters who is asking. The name was never as accepted as they had believed, and that was likely limiting their customer base.

The rebranding process involved months of collecting input and testing ideas until a winning name emerged: "Faubourg." This French word is often used in New Orleans to describe "surrounding neighborhoods." Jim's voice fills with excitement as he explains how the new name aligns with their inclusive strategy. "New Orleans is not just Bourbon Street, there are so many cultures here, and this name captures that." He tells me about their Pride Month celebrations, their employment training of local black and brown young people for a career in learning how to serve beer, and their highlighting of nontouristy stories of the Mardi Gras Indians. "This is part of who Faubourg is," he says. As he later wrote in the *Harvard Business Review,* "We want to make a product that brings people together, not one that pulls them apart."[1]

Many people fear that names, traditions, brands, and mascots cannot survive dramatic change. Jim believes otherwise. "I think consumers have a twenty-four-month memory," he surmises, citing well-known national brand debacles that I had long forgotten (for example, food poisoning outbreaks at Chipotle) to illustrate his point. In fact, he sees opportunities for brands to revitalize their values and customers. When the *Harvard Business Review* asked Jim to offer advice to a fictional brand named Overseer Whiskey, he wrote, "[The company] could do nothing, but that would almost certainly limit its whiskey's appeal to an ever-smaller segment of customers as modern societal norms prompt people to avoid products with problematic pasts. . . . Just because 42%

of whiskey drinkers don't know that the word 'overseer' has connections to slavery isn't a reason to do nothing."

Jim sees the new name as an opportunity. It has prompted reflection and catalyzed action. When he describes how the company is engaging a wider demographic in their community, he wonders, "I'm not sure we would have been doing all these things as Dixie." Maybe the name change is revitalizing the company's way of engaging with the community, or maybe the company's way of engaging with the community is revitalizing the name. Maybe both are true. Taking responsibility is an opportunity to be forward-looking in what we do. We have the same opportunity in the words we choose.

Interrogation of the "Small" Things

In Chapter 4, we examined tools to help us connect the dots. One of those was the connection between our thoughts and our language. Language seeps into our thoughts and vice versa, making it important to interrogate the "small things," such as our choice of words, as we saw in the renaming of Dixie Beer.

In *Caste: The Origins of Our Discontents,* Isabel Wilkerson interrogates language.[2] At the start of the book, she announces that she will deliberately avoid customary language such as "racism" and "white supremacy." "Our era requires new language," she explains to a *Washington Post* reporter.[3] She uses terms such as "upper caste" to describe white Americans and "lower caste" to describe black Americans, arguing that our American social system is more similar than different to those of India and Nazi Germany. She believes the linguistic shift leads to a mental shift, offering readers a "surprising and arresting wide-angle reframing."

This approach echoes Susan Neiman's advice in *Learning from the Germans: Race and the Memory of Evil.* She writes, "What can other countries learn from the German experience? To look at your own country as if it were a foreign one. It's crucial to have a broken relationship to your past, to be ready to see your own history with shame and horror."[4]

Similarly, Edward Baptist avoids gauzy words like *plantations* in his book *The Half Has Never Been Told: Slavery and the Making of American Capitalism,* in favor of "labor camps."[5] Like a growing number of historians, he writes "enslavers" instead of the more legitimizing term "slave owners." Old language reinforces old ways of thinking.

In this book, I mostly avoid using the words *slave* and *slave owner.* I have tried instead to use *enslaved person, enslaver,* and *person who enslaved humans,* as many contemporary academics and activists have convinced me is more accurate.[6] The usual terminology normalizes the institution of slavery, allowing us to "forget" that humans enslaving other humans was not an inevitability, but the result of deliberate decisions. The noun *slave* creates a semblance that the entirety of the individual's humanity is captured in their state of enslavement. True, changing terminology is tricky because the historical terms are pervasive. While speech habits are hard to change, the rationale seems straightforward.

Less straightforward is the scrutiny of language used to describe something unrelated to slavery. For example, I use the word *master* frequently. I refer to the master bedroom in my home, the master document when collaborating with coauthors, and the headmaster at my children's schools. I am affiliated with universities that used to have a house master in the residential colleges; I have two master's degrees. It is standard in computer programming[7] to refer to different database structures as master and slave. My sense is not that the word *master* needs to disappear, but that the word *master* as used in certain contexts is directly linked—the dots connect—to its slavery connotation. Additionally, the male-gendered word has sexist connotations (for both reasons, many in the real estate industry have shifted to using "primary bedroom" rather than "master bedroom"). Context and words matter.

Interrogating these "small things" matters. This means tuning in, not out, when someone raises a concern about language. This means listening with open ears rather than rolling one's eyes when we are corrected.

This means digging through the basement of this old American house before declaring everything to be okay. Some of the uses will stay, some will go. We will discover some clear-cut problems. No doubt, changing language is difficult. We will trip over our words for longer than we like. And then, our usage habits will evolve because language always evolves. Some of us grew up saying "neato" or "dyno-mite," after all; we need not use the same words forever. While small changes to our language are not all that is needed, they are a step toward taking responsibility.

Hard to Say I'm Sorry

Apologies are another way to take responsibility. Research says that apologies matter.[8] Effective apologies share several features, including sincerity and responsibility-taking.[9] Ineffective apologies come across as insincere, face-saving, and/or deflecting responsibility. These ineffective apologies deepen the harm and damage the relationship, perhaps as harmful or more harmful than a lack of apology.

Public apologies carry extra weight. A public apology declares rightness and wrongness, claims collective responsibility, and recognizes collective injustice. Political scientist Melissa Nobles notes that the pace of public apologies and gestures of regret accelerated in the second half of the twentieth century; half of these apologies were connected to World War II.[10] Many were issued in the 1990s, amid the fifty-year anniversary of the war. I suspect these commemorations fueled an increase in collective demands and collective guilt. Without the apology, there is no moral stand.

While an apology may appear to look backward, research shows that it is actually received as a commitment for the future. The apology signals a reset, with the spoken or unspoken promise that the future will be different than the past. Similar to taking out the garbage from the kitchen, we not only get rid of stuff from earlier, we also clear space for now and later.

Examples abound. The queen of England offered sympathy for England's role in the famine in Ireland.[11] The Vatican apologized for its persecution of Galileo[12] and its inaction in the Holocaust.[13] The Australian government apologized for the harm done to indigenous peoples. The U.S. government has apologized in some form for its maltreatment of Japanese-Americans, Native Americans, and the Tuskegee syphilis study victims.

Still, the United States government has yet to apologize for slavery. Over the years, the House of Representatives and Senate have proposed various resolutions apologizing for slavery but have failed to pass a joint bill. The absence of the apology is puzzling. Apologies are a "strong and cheap device to restore social or economic relationships that have been disturbed" and when they are not forthcoming, victims often seek punishment.[14] In some ways, this bare minimum of an apology is simply expected—like toothbrushing—but not grounds for celebration or congratulation. Nonetheless, no apology has been offered. That which should be a given becomes ground for a senseless battle. The absence of an apology, especially when the culpability is obvious, is harmful because it suggests that there is no garbage to be taken out, despite the odor.

In *How the Word Is Passed: A Reckoning with the History of Slavery Across America,* Clint Smith speaks with Hasan Kane, a history teacher in Senegal, a country pillaged by colonialism that became a central site of the slave trade. Hasan wants an apology from the government. His stance is that just as an apology without compensation is insufficient, compensation without an apology is problematic. The apology is what Smith calls "moral compensation." Without the moral compensation, Hasan feared that the mindset would become, in Smith's words, " 'Okay. Now you received money. We repaired everything. Don't talk about it anymore.' "

As with all systemic issues, in societies or old houses, there is rarely a single solution. When there is a long-standing roof leak, the roof will surely need to be fixed, and so will the walls, floors, property, foundation, gutters, insulation, and window frames. There is no "one and done." Both big things and small things matter.

We Hold People Accountable . . . Sometimes

While taking responsibility for an old house is intuitive, taking responsibility for our country is less so. For example, the majority of white Americans oppose the idea of reparations for slavery.[15] In 2011, anti-white bias was seen as more prevalent than anti-black bias among white Americans. The data proving this to be incorrect is robust. Based on the Marley Hypothesis research mentioned in Chapter 4, this phenomenon may be due in part to a lack of knowledge about the events of the past and the impact of the past on the present.

In her 2020 *New York Times Magazine* cover story "What Is Owed," Nikole Hannah-Jones argues that we have failed to grasp the economic dimension of slavery.[16] "At the time of the Civil War, the value of the enslaved human beings held as property added up to more than all of this nation's railroads and factories combined. And yet, enslaved people saw not a dime of this wealth. They owned nothing and were owed nothing from all that had been built from their toil," she writes. Slavery, she argues, was economic exploitation. When slavery ended, our government compensated people who had enslaved other humans for their loss of "property" after emancipation, but never compensated those who were actually enslaved for their labor and its fruits.

Even the clichéd forty acres and a mule never actually happened.[17] This is another fable I long believed. When General William T. Sherman signed Special Field Order 15, this decree set aside 400,000 acres of Confederate land for freed slaves, as well as leftover army mules. Before the end of the year, President Andrew Johnson reversed the decree and returned the land to the people who'd enslaved humans and had originally owned the land.

When it came to those who attacked our country on September 11, 2001, we pursued accountability. When we incarcerate more of our population than most countries, we claim this is because of accountability. So, we are not against accountability.

But we simply offered mass immunity for human trafficking, kidnapping, enslavement, torture, wage theft, and rape. We never called it mass immunity. We just acted as if it did not happen. We did not take responsibility. Slavery . . . no accountability. Jim Crow . . . no accountability. Lynchings . . . no accountability.[18]

The Case for Reparations

Before Ta-Nehisi Coates was a bestselling author, he spent two years working on a single article for *The Atlantic* magazine: "The Case for Reparations."[19] It is obvious that whites and blacks are not proportionately distributed by geography, occupation, income, education, health care, legal treatment, or any other feature of modern life. The disparities are stark and pervasive. Coates focused on one: housing in Chicago. The article went viral[20] and exploded into a national conversation in 2014, eventually leading to him testifying before Congress.

When the article first came out, it was widely praised on social media and in conversations with people I respect. Accordingly, I did not do my usual on-screen skim. This article was long and important, so I printed it and set it aside to read when I could give it the time and space it deserved. I lost track of where that first printout landed. I printed it again, and scrawled in red Sharpie marker NEED TO READ.

We moved recently and when I did the dreaded excavation of my home office, I discovered a total of four printouts of that article. Each one was stapled carefully, with a sticky exclaiming its importance, stashed away until the right time came for me to give it the required attention. I kept thinking about reading the article, yet not actually reading it.

Eventually, a few years later, I read the article. While I am embarrassed, I now recognize why I resisted reading it for so long. The case for reparations is clear-cut in my mind but the logistics of reparations feel intractable. Why learn about something that feels both essential and impossible? Why go into the basement if you're afraid you can't fix what you find? My problem was not a knowledge gap, but a pragmatism gap.

When I finally read the article, I realized my error. Like Hannah-Jones, Coates argues that we are missing the point when talking about the oppression of African-Americans. "Behind all of that oppression was actually theft," he says. "This is not just mean. This is not just maltreatment. This is the theft of resources out of that community." And, because of the history in housing and "virtually every institution with some degree of history in America, be it public, be it private [of] extracting wealth and resources out of the African-American community," he concludes that there is a case for reparations.

What are reparations? No amount of money can compensate for the stolen humanity, lives, and joy. However, economic exploitation can be quantified. Most people associate reparations with a big blanket check. But Coates argues that reparations should be highly specific, pegged to actual harmful policies and quantifiable harm. In order to compute that amount, build that awareness, and garner that support, other steps also have to happen.

This is the point where Coates really got me. The key is to determine what harm was done. Until we start that process, debating what is practical or what is "a long time ago" is premature. We first need to tabulate and reckon with the harm. The work precedes reparations and there is no reasonable rationale for not doing it. Before we can repair the house, we must determine what actually needs repair. As one does with plumbers and painters, we first need to assess the damage before we can get an estimate.

True, no words, dollars, or policies would be sufficient. True, there is no way to satisfy all the interests. Then again, the same was also true with 9/11 victims. Yet Congress still implemented the September 11th Victim Compensation Fund, even when the perpetrators were foreign, unlike with slavery. Perhaps it is because there is no complicity to admit or responsibility to take that we are able to take action when the enemy is foreign.

Start by Studying the Issue

When a city, state, or country assembles a committee to "study" reparations, we might be tempted to roll our eyes. Another committee, another study, another waste of time. But this is necessary work. We have so much to (un)learn. We need to see the problem, embrace paradox, connect the dots and reject fables in order to take responsibility. Pragmatic solutions will be needed, but not until we clarify the problem we are solving.

To move forward, we must get specific. We can no longer bemoan the abstraction of redlining; we must determine what specifically happened in our towns and neighborhoods. We can no longer flail our arms at the intergenerational wealth gap; we have to determine whose grandparents were ineligible for Social Security. In other words, we must reckon with our whitewashed past.

Consider the city of Evanston, Illinois.[21] Evanston received national media attention in the spring of 2021 as the first city in the United States to attempt reparations. They "acknowledge[d] the harm caused to African-American/Black Evanston residents due to discriminatory housing policies and practices and inaction on the part of the City from 1919–1969." At first blush, this program seemed to be setting a template for other cities by uncovering and addressing a specific act of harm.

But problems arose in the initial phase. Evanston has 12,000 black residents. The program would provide noncash payments of $25,000 to only sixteen of them, excluding more than 99 percent of residents and ignoring those who had previously lived (or whose ancestors had lived) in Evanston. Many of those residents felt the program architects had not sought community input. The lack of input from those affected is a common critique of reparations attempts, and suggests a need to invest more time, money, and effort studying the issue more carefully rather than rushing to disburse payments. That said, this is only Phase 1 of their plan.

One might be critical of Evanston for what they did, or what they did not do, or for what they tried to do. But here is what I see: I see residents doing the work of reckoning with the whitewashed past and trying to decolonize their systems. I see residents who know more than they did before. And I see those as necessary first steps. No doubt, there is much to be learned from those who go first.

Reparations can take many forms, from direct payments to enhanced opportunities. They can be pinpointed for descendants or provided to a broader population experiencing the legacy of slavery. The process will not be easy. It will sometimes feel for naught. It will sometimes lead to embarrassing media coverage. It may lead to a flood of lawsuits. We should prepare for those possibilities. This is a moment for being good-ish, not good, which means being open to learning and growth, even when—especially when—we are feeling proud of the good deeds we are doing.

Cautionary Note

There is a risk here that we will confuse documenting harm with repairing harm or mistake changing a name for changing a policy. Taking a step in the right direction feels satisfying. But there is also the possibility—what psychologists call moral licensing[22]—that we will take that step and then stop moving. Much like when one turns off online notifications and works productively on Monday morning, only to go down the distraction rabbit hole Monday afternoon because "I earned it" (look in the mirror, Dr. Chugh!), the same psychology can take hold here. Taking responsibility requires ongoing effort, not a one-and-done approach, however tempting. Study and documentation are a necessary but not sufficient starting point . . . not an endpoint. The temptation to declare ourselves noble and the work done is seductive but deceptive.

Taking responsibility is sometimes tumultuous. We are seeing the occasional apology or reparation, and the ensuing debates. We are arguing about what it means to decolonize our language, our minds, and our culture. We are fighting about what should be in our textbooks and our classrooms. We are building museums, erecting memorials, and installing markers. We are excavating primary sources and historical artifacts to reveal the truth about what really happened. We are poking around in the basement of this old house, and pushing aside those blocking the door. To continue taking responsibility, we are going to need to build some grit.

– 7 –

Build Grit

*At some point it is no longer a question of whether
we can learn this history but whether we have the
collective will to reckon with it.*
—CLINT SMITH

Oh Myyy

"Tuck in your shirt," one giggling daughter said. "Straighten your legs, Mom," cajoled my other giggling daughter, while filming me on her phone. In the quarantine summer of 2020, I found my fifty-two-year-old self trying to revive the glory and abs of my youth. I was in the yard doing my first cartwheel in decades and it showed. My neighbors were amused.

It all started when I decided to aim for the stars and ask George Takei if I could interview him for this book. George is beloved by fans across the globe for multiple reasons. In the 1960s, he starred in the original cast of one of the largest media franchises in history: *Star Trek*. Today, decades later, tens of millions of social media followers enjoy his quirky sense of humor and strong political views, making him a leading influencer. In recent years he has become known for the catchphrase "oh myyy," due to an uncomfortable moment captured on *The Howard Stern Show*. George is the quintessential American celebrity, still shaping pop culture sixty years after he first entered its spotlight.

My request for an interview was facilitated by a mutual contact and a glib, attention-grabbing promise: "I will do cartwheels if you say yes!" To my delighted surprise, he wrote back, jokingly saying he would love to see my cartwheel. So here we were. We ended the video with my arms reaching for the sky, exclaiming, "We love you, George." I plugged in the heating pad as I hit send, hoping my gymnastic display would clinch the interview. It did! When I reached him by phone, George opened our conversation by singing me my theme song, "Hello, Dolly!" Few moments in my life have delighted me so.

A Euphemism for Prison

While George's work is widely known, his extraordinary life story may not be as well known. Born in Los Angeles in 1937, George was the happy child of his mother (born in Sacramento) and his father (born in Japan but raised in the United States). His parents owned and operated a thriving dry-cleaning business.

When George was four years old, he heard banging on his front door. The house trembled from the heavy pounding. His father told him to quickly get dressed. George saw tears rolling down his mother's cheeks. Eighty years later, it is a moment he says he cannot forget.

Later, he would understand that the United States had entered a global war with Japan, Germany, and Italy, leading President Franklin Delano Roosevelt to issue Executive Order 9066. As a result, 120,000 people of Japanese ancestry, 11,000 people of German ancestry, and 3,000 people of Italian ancestry were removed from their homes and placed in internment camps. The majority were American citizens, including George's family. After a lifetime of hard work, they were forced to surrender their two-bedroom home and their dry-cleaning business and placed in a "single, smelly horse stall" at a local racetrack. George recalls it as a painful and humiliating experience.

His family was then tagged, like cattle, and transported to the Rohwer War Relocation Center in Arkansas, where all adults were told to sign a "loyalty pledge," with two particularly controversial questions. One asked if the individual would bear arms to defend the nation. George recalls, "This is being asked of my mother to bear arms and defend the United States of America, which meant that she was being asked to abandon her children [three children under six] to bear arms to defend the nation that's imprisoning her family. It was preposterous."

The second question also felt like a trap, asking if the respondent would swear loyalty to the United States of America and forswear loyalty to the emperor of Japan. In other words, it presumed an existing loyalty to the emperor. "My mother was born in Sacramento!" George explains the dilemma his parents faced. "If you answered no, I don't have a loyalty to the emperor to forswear, then does that not also apply to the loyalty to the United States?" It was a test of allegiance with no right answer and a guaranteed failing grade. After George's parents answered no to both questions, they were taken to an internment camp in California with three layers of barbed wire, machine gun towers, and rows of tanks heavily guarding the perimeter. Before George was old enough to go to kindergarten, he was a prisoner.

Like most euphemisms, "internment camp" leaves a different impression than the reality captured in first-person accounts by George and many others. The term is not commonly used in everyday language and rings softer than *incarcerate, jail,* or *imprison,* terms that also apply here. Euphemisms are often an indication that social identity threat is on high alert; we are trying to bring the threat down.

It is also curious that the phrase "internment camp" is used almost exclusively to refer to the mass imprisonment of Japanese-Americans during World War II. The English word *internment* originated from the French word *interner,* which means "send to the interior, confine," and the dictionary definition of *intern* is to "confine or impound especially during a war," as in to "intern enemy aliens."[1] The literal meaning of locking up enemies during war is inaccurate; the majority of the 120,000 Japanese-Americans who were locked up were American citizens, not enemies of the state. The difference between internment and incarceration seemed to be that those in the internment camps were imprisoned for a crime they might commit in the future, not one they supposedly committed in the past.

"I wasn't an alien," George says. "I was a young boy. I was born in Los Angeles." Hearing George's firsthand story helps us unpack the home team bias that has whitewashed our understanding of how we treated fellow Americans during a time of war . . . and how the home team was not all of the American team.

George and his family were imprisoned for three years. When they were released, the U.S. government offered them no reparation and no resources to rebuild their lives, outside of twenty-five dollars and a train ticket. Their business, life savings, and home were gone. Nothing was returned. They were homeless and jobless.

Imagine This in Your Own Family

Like George's dad, I was a baby when my parents brought me to the United States; I have no memories of living anywhere else. I am an American citizen, as are my parents. They have lived here longer than they lived in India (by decades). My husband has a similar story. Our children were born in the United States and have never lived anywhere else.

Imagine if the United States and India went to war. Imagine the government ordering my family to abandon our jobs, our homes, our bank accounts. With the executive order like the one FDR signed, we would be deemed aliens in our own land. I would have to abandon New York University, my students, and my research. My husband would have to abandon the patients—some elderly, some ill—in his medical practice. Our lifetime of careful savings would be erased. We would be moved far away from our home in New York. Our children would be pulled from their schools. We would be imprisoned indefinitely, behind barbed wire and soldiers with guns. There would be no trial or due process by which we could prove our innocence or highlight that we have pledged allegiance, paid taxes, and proudly voted our entire lives. I ask you to imagine this because wrinkles in time make events a long time ago look blurry. Events in the present, or imagined future, help us unmute our emotional reactions and overcome the Long-Time-Ago Illusion. Imagining this allows us to empathize with what George and so many others experienced. Also, it helps us overcome the hindsight bias in which what happened seems inevitable rather than preventable.

Allegiance

After recovering from the delight of being serenaded by Captain Sulu, I ask George about his obvious deep love for his country and fierce patriotism. After all, George Takei's family was not treated fairly or well by the United States government. To my surprise, he speaks of FDR, the man "who put us behind those barbed wire fences," as a "great president." George recalls Roosevelt's boldness and political creativity in the face of a horrific depression, his reminder that the only thing we have to fear is fear itself. "He built bridges, roads, and post offices, and thought of the entire spectrum of society, including artists who are the first to be unemployed, and gave them jobs."

"Still," George observes, "even that man is a fallible human being. He got stampeded by Pearl Harbor and the racism that swept across this country. He really didn't know that much about Asian-Americans or specifically Japanese-Americans. And so it was easy for him to get swept up like that. Our democracy is dependent on the capacity for greatness that the people have, but it is as vulnerable as human fallibility." I hear George using the tools I am writing about. He is embracing the paradox of FDR. He is connecting the dots of what happened then and what is happening now with how we treat the undocumented, the immigrant, the nonwhite. He is rejecting fables of idyllic internment camps.

I also hear the Marley Hypothesis. The gap that George observes is in Roosevelt's knowledge. He explains: "If we're going to be responsible participants in a people's democracy, we need to know our history of fallibility as well as the great achievements." This motivation was critical in his determination to bring the story of the internment camps to the broader public through speaking engagements, his bestselling graphic memoir *They Called Us Enemy,* board leadership of the Japanese American National Museum in Los Angeles, and the Broadway musical *Allegiance,* based on his life story.

Gritty Patriots

When I witness George's ability to appreciate both the reality of our country's mistakes and the grandeur of our country's greatness, I see a lesson in loving with a broken heart. He can describe Roosevelt as a great president despite the harm done to the Takei family and so many others. He can see America as a great country despite the terrible things that have happened in America. I ask him how he embraces those paradoxes.

"Well, the alternative, given my childhood imprisonment, is a sense of victimhood and that is not a productive thing," he says. "The opportunity here is that our democracy provides us with the opportunity to participate in it. In fact, it demands that as our responsibility." George's love seems to fuel and be fueled by his grit.

Psychologist Angela Duckworth defines grit as passion and perseverance for long-term and meaningful goals.[2] Grit enables us to do hard things that we care about. Perseverance is what keeps us engaged with an endeavor even when we fail or when challenges keep popping up. Passion keeps us coming back to a project, sacrificing less compelling demands on our time. Long-term and meaningful goals allow us to commit to something we find both worthy and challenging over multiple years. Measures of grit include questions about overcoming setbacks to conquer an important challenge, maintaining focus on projects that take more than a few months to complete, and diligence.

Imagine if we were to treat love of country as a project that requires grit, instead of a birthright or entitlement. Patriotism would be something we earned, not wore. Gritty patriots would be those who showed both passion and perseverance for the long-term, meaningful goal of a country in which every person is created equal and there is justice for all. Many people have the passion—the flags, the songs, the red-white-and-blue T-shirts. But fewer people have the perseverance. Loving your country with passion but not perseverance is more like the newlywed variety of love, all crepes and cuddles. We need the middle-aged variety, with its aging mix of comfort, belonging, regret, commitment, and deep hard-earned love. George Takei exemplifies the gritty patriot.

Entitled to Easy Love

We can all recognize entitlement. A "bridezilla" who sees her big day as immune from Murphy's law. A vacationer who ignores the impact of their partying on local residents. A colleague quick to schedule days off but slow to cover the workload of others out sick. A commuter who cuts the line with little regard for those who have been waiting their turn. George believes we are not entitled to democracy.

Researchers define "psychological entitlement" as the "stable and pervasive sense that one deserves more and is entitled to more than others."[3] While psychological entitlement can be a personality trait (and I suspect we each can summon a list of names with this trait), it can also be prompted by circumstance. For example, in one study, researchers were able to evoke more entitled behavior by subconsciously exposing study participants to words like *special, better, superior, deserve,* and *more.*[4] Each of us may be prone to feeling more (or less) entitled based on our circumstances. We see ourselves as deserving more than others and tend to disparage others, so that we see them as less deserving.

How do we square this notion of entitlement with the belief that I—and many others—hold that America is the greatest country in the world? After all, I am the child of immigrants who chose to come to the United States because they saw and still see it as the greatest country in the world. The idea that our country is both exceptional and an exception is called American exceptionalism.[5] In this belief system, the United States is superior to other nations and unique in its superiority, a shining city on a hill. Being an American means one is entitled to having that shining city as your home address. Debates rage on whether America is exceptional, but those debates are not my interest here. My interest is how that entitled view inhibits our ability to love our country fully.

There is much to love about the United States and its history. No doubt, it would be easier if we could love all of it, if the story was prettier, cleaner, more consistent. But are we entitled to that ease, devoid of paradox or ambivalence? I have noticed that we have an expectation, possibly unconscious, about how our country should make us feel that we do not assume to be true for people in other countries. We expect our country to always make us feel good about our love for it, without holding the same expectations for people who live in Cuba or Germany or South Africa. We expect that loving our country means we will always like it. We feel entitled to a world in which the good guys win and in which we are always the good guys. We feel entitled to having our consistency cravings satisfied. This sense of entitlement makes us less likely to do the work we need to do to create a more just future for our country. Sometimes our country, this country we love, breaks our heart.

Loving with a Broken Heart

Psychologist Albert Bandura once wrote, "The capacity to exercise control over the nature and quality of one's life is the essence of humanness."[6] Psychologists call this capacity agency. An agency mindset consists of efficacy (the belief that one is capable of making a difference), optimism (the belief that one can make a difference in the future), and imagination (the capacity to see a range of situations where one can make a difference).[7] When we see ourselves as agents, we can make active choices, rather than be acted upon. We can shape the world, the thoughts within us, and the people by us.

We see such active choosing in George Takei. He does not view himself as entitled to an idyllic history or comforting fable. Instead he recognizes his agency to love and criticize his country. He does not view the nation as a completed project, and he views his role as participating in its next steps.

After all, if we view our country as done, what work is there left to do? With our broken heart comes the opportunity to improve things. Dewy eyes early in a relationship are fun for the high, but not instructive for welding spending habits, temperature preferences, and needs for alone time into a sustainable relationship. We can love more fully and thus build the country we want to live with.

George illustrates that loving with a broken heart is not a passive activity. It is active. It is like trying another password when the first one didn't work, and then another, and then clicking the link and jumping through CAPTCHA hoops to set a new one. It is distracting the puppy from the chair leg she loves to chew and then distracting her again, and then moving the chair, and then buying her new chew toys. It is applying for grad school and getting rejected, and taking a test prep course and testing again, and applying again, and practicing for your interview, and being accepted off the waitlist. We take this kind of active, persistent stance in so many parts of our lives. When it comes to forgotten passwords, chewing puppies, and rejected applications, we do what needs to be done. We can adopt the same attitude with our country. We can face what we do not like and do not want and can barely believe. And then, we can do better.

Loving with a broken heart does not mean that what broke your heart did not happen or was an aberration. It does not mean that you ignore or deny reality. That may avoid a broken heart, but it also avoids a full heart. A conditional heart will only love a perfect union, rather than a more perfect union. A full heart loves the beautiful and the broken. This is a fierce kind of love, the kind that will not turn away or be deceived. It is not easy love, but it is the fullest kind of love.

This kind of love reminds me of a poem, "The Invitation," by Oriah Mountain Dreamer. The narrator describes a gutting night filled with grief and despair and asks if you can rise the next morning, exhausted, and be there for the children.[8] Our love of country can come from a place much like our indefatigable love of our children. At times there will be grief and despair. At times we will feel bruised to the bone. And, still, we will get up and do what needs to be done.

How to Build Grit

The Character Lab website proposes three ways to encourage grit in others: to model it, celebrate it, and enable it.[9] These suggestions work well for our purposes. We can share our learnings with others, expressing both satisfaction and frustration as we learn more. We can celebrate those who are digging in. We can be supportive of people who are struggling to understand and face what they did not know.

To model grit, we need to build our own. One way to increase our own grit is to tap into the meaning of what we are trying to do. Duckworth and colleagues have shown that an orientation toward pursuing meaning predicts grittiness.[10] When we reflect on the purpose of unlearning and relearning of American history and how it contributes to society, we will put in more effort, withstand more challenges, and enjoy the process more.

Again, grit is perseverance plus passion. Duckworth writes, "What ripens passion is the conviction that your work matters." It is important for us to understand our country's past. We love this country. We care about its future. We care about our children's and grandchildren's future in this country. We care about democracy. We care about equality. We care about unity. Reminding ourselves that these things matter—the power of values affirmation—helps keep us gritty.

Organizational scholars Amy Wrzesniewski and Jane Dutton showed the importance of connecting to what matters to us in their study of hospital cleaners.[11] Those who attached meaning to their work—contributing to patients' health and the hospital's functioning—engaged in the work differently than those who saw no higher purpose in their daily tasks. By crafting the task as one with this higher purpose, they recrafted the tasks themselves.

In other words, reckoning with our past is not learning for learning's sake (though there is nothing wrong with that) or a fool's errand. Unlearning whitewashed history is an intentional pursuit of truth that will help us be the country and patriots we mean to be. We have met many a gritty patriot—in trainer Meghan Lydon, the educators of Zionsville, Indiana, Mayor Mitch Landrieu, icon George Takei. They are clear about what they value and why. Meaning boosters keep them in gritty patriot mode.

So, maybe it is not too late for us to unlearn. Maybe it is not too late to reckon. Maybe it is not too late to see the problem and take responsibility. Then and now, now and then, let us begin. Together, we will discover that what we fear will hurt, divide, and confuse us will actually bring us closer. We will finally be watching the same screen, seeing the same story, and understanding the same nation. We will understand each other better. We will understand ourselves better. We will love our land. And, as gritty patriots, we will fight for a more just future.

Many people believe America is the greatest country on earth. You may be one of those people. If that is the case, then you also believe Americans can do hard things. Unlearning whitewashed history is hard. Decolonizing our minds is hard. But it is not as hard as we think it will be and we, as Americans, are stronger than we realize. We can do this. We can love our country and know all its stories. We can move forward by looking back. We can learn and unlearn. We can reckon with our past and build a more just future.

Epilogue

Our House

We began the journey at a little house on a prairie, with my downfall from smug parent to shortsighted patriot. Our little kids are now teenagers tethered to their rooms and phones. Looking back, I am grateful for those hours reading aloud and those days traveling together.

I am also stunned at how fully they absorbed the stories they heard. When I look at their old school papers, I see drawings and anecdotes of *Little House* and the Ingalls family sprinkled throughout their artwork and writing in kindergarten and first grade. One of our daughters dressed up as Laura Ingalls in the first-grade Favorite Character Parade, alongside Pinkalicious and Junie B. Jones. I poured stories of this lovely family and their colonizing of our land into my children and those stories became the knowledge in their blood as they grew into young people. I have grown along with them, even because of them.

In this past decade, the world has been on fire, with unlearning opportunities flying like sparks around us. Our kids, like many kids, are fired up for social change. They have that young person's blessed combination of optimism and cynicism, which bubbles into action. They do not seem to be suffering from shame and guilt. They have less belief grief to navigate. They are ahead of us adults.

Recently, one of our kids wrote a poem[1] for school that she showed us only after submitting it. Here is an excerpt:

The psychic wound of racism[2]
Resulted in inevitable wounds
In the land
And the country itself.[3]

central park wasn't always
the wealthy new york child's playground.
it was a Black Oasis.
it was Seneca Village.

the Sawatch Range wasn't always
the place wealthy new york kids escaped to.
it was the mountain sand dunes,
it was (and still is) the home of the Ute people.

a false "destiny"
a sense of entitlement
a need for more privilege
people stole this land
stole homes
stole livelihoods.

now recreating in these places
i read the signs
i acknowledge the land
but it is not enough.
it will never be enough.
so what's next?

I do not know where she learned this. Did I tell her about how a thriving black community known as Seneca Village was razed to create Central Park? Maybe. Did I teach her about false destinies? Doubtful.

Still, someone did. This kind of learning and unlearning results from someone's intentional effort. Teachers, and content creators, and authors, and activists, and historians, and artists, journalists, and TikTokers, and witness bearers, and storytellers in Hollywood, and so many others . . . they are probably teaching our kids and helping them unlearn what I taught them. These reckoners are teaching us all. I thank them.

On my end, I suspect that all those truth-telling books I have been reading and my willingness to unlearn over recent years have seeped into the family water supply. I can take credit for that, at least. I have gone from the Little House on the Prairie to the old house with the basement, gathering tools along the way. In the end, it is our house, all of it.

There is much my kids doubt about me—my sense of humor, my cooking, my ability to stay up past eleven. But I do not think they will ever doubt how much I love my country . . . even when I do not always like what happens in my country, even when I am mad at this country, even when I critique this country. I love my country like I love them—unconditionally, with my eyes open. My husband and I have always told our children that there is no problem we are not willing to see, no dilemma they cannot bring to us, no mistake we cannot reckon with, no obstacle we do not have the grit to face . . . as long as they tell the truth and take responsibility.

I hope they believe us. And I hope you believe me. We can love with a broken heart. We can do hard things. We can make things better. We can build a more just future.

That is the most American mindset ever.

Acknowledgments

First and foremost, my teachings in this book are often my learnings from others. My intent has been to cite them with care and amplify their work with my curation of stories and science.

I started this book in the summer of 2019. George Floyd was alive. Donald Trump lived in the White House. Coronavirus was not in our national vocabulary. While the world changed a great deal over the course of writing this book, the support I received from many people did not.

I am very grateful to those who shared their stories and work with me by phone or Zoom: Jim Birch, Hazel Gurland-Pooler, Michael Harriot, Mitch Landrieu, Meghan Lydon, "Sidney Norman," Wendy Smith, George Takei, Jeanne Theoharis, and Pamela Toler. Their interviews have been lightly edited for clarity and flow. I hope I have done their words and stories justice.

Several brilliant friends spent hours reading early drafts and trusted me with their feedback. Thank you to Cinque Henderson, Lorri Perkins, and Jeff Wilser. The book is better because of their significant investment of time and thought. I wish I had the talent to deliver on all of the amazing suggestions they offered. Chances are the parts you liked were made better by the suggestions they made.

I am grateful for support, introductions, conversations, and/or suggestions from Daniel Braunfeld, Gail Bruno, Eugene Caruso, Marla Felcher, Ileana Ferreras, Antonia Garcia, Emily Heaphy, Karim Kassam, Jay Kuo, Alex Lacamoire, Joe Magee, Dave Nussbaum, Betsy Levy Paluck, Eliza Parrilla, Aneeta Rattan, Todd Rogers, Brent Rosso, Monique Rugile, Becky Schaumberg, Devna Shukla, Katie Sutton, Tom Stuart, Jamie Tobias, and Jenn Wynn.

Keith Meatto has been a wonderful thought partner, teacher, and freelance external editor. The book is far better because of his expert pen. If you need someone to elevate your writing and thinking, I cannot recommend him enough. Serena Saxena provided careful proofreading at a critical moment under pressure.

I asked a few of my personal heroes to read the manuscript and consider an endorsement. Their time, interest, and words honor me deeply. Thank you, Uché Blackstock, Angela Duckworth, Michael Bungay Stanier, and Kenji Yoshino. Daniela Segura provided extensive support with references while Morgan Powers, and Amanda Pung did a lifesaving proofread. I appreciate their painstaking and patient efforts.

I thank Sabrina Burse at Belay Virtual Assistants for showing me what is possible when I becomes we. This marks an important new chapter in how I work.

My newsletter—*Dear Good People*—has been a companion project to this one. Katie Sutton, Evelyn Parker, and Belinda Li have been central to this labor of love.

Danielle Kolodkin at the HarperCollins Speakers Bureau has been a valued speaking agent during a complicated time. I appreciate her commitment to bringing my work to a broad range of audiences.

My wonderful colleagues at the New York University Stern School of Business (especially within the Management and Organizations Department) exemplify collegiality and collaboration. I am especially grateful for the support of my department chair, Steve Blader. I also thank the dean's office and our public affairs team.

Special thanks to the staff at the Comfort Suites in Bozeman, Montana, where a brief solo writing retreat did wonders for my motivation, focus, and creativity.

Mahzarin Banaji remains the pinnacle of intellect married with purpose. I feel so lucky to be mentored/inspired by her and to be part of the Banaji Lab community.

The "No Club"—my dear friends Modupe Akinola and Katy Milkman—are the wisest and most loving of "sisters."

"WELD"—Wanda Holland Greene, Eliza Armstrong, Lisa Carnoy— inspire me with their brilliant heads, hearts, and souls.

The Women of Organizational Behavior group, founded by Katy DeCelles, shows what a web-based community can be at its best. The WOB Writer's Retreats have far exceeded my expectations, offering not just Pomodoros but also love and laughter.

BLING, founded by Zoe Chance, is filled with inspiring authors and generous spirits.

Rena Seltzer has had a profound impact on how I write and work. Neither of my books would exist without her coaching and her excellent book, *The Coach's Guide for Women Professors* (in my view, it is not just for women or professors).

Max Bazerman is a mentor, friend, and great human. He has done more good for more people than anyone I know in my field, and I am one of those people. I will never stop feeling lucky to have him in my life. And the Bazerman Non-Lab will be a lifelong community of learning, love, and laughter.

Leila Campoli, of Stonesong, remains my dream literary agent. Meeting her on my birthday in 2016 has been the birthday gift that keeps giving. I consider myself so fortunate to be represented by her and to be in a world where she is helping birth so many wonderful books. And her weekly writing sessions are a stimulating joy and a source of camaraderie.

My editor, Stephanie Hitchcock, and I have now worked on two books together. I am so grateful for the trust she has put in my ideas and intuitions from day one in 2016 at HarperBusiness and now at the

Atria imprint of Simon & Schuster. Her intellectual and structural suggestions always elevate the quality of my work. She is fighting the good fight, day after day, page after page.

Alejandra Rocha at Atria Books shared editorial insights well beyond her years through direct and developmental notes on multiple drafts. What a smart and promising talent! I am excited to see her career unfold and have no doubt that I will be bragging that I knew her when.

Sean Delone at Atria Books was with this project early on and helped it get its start.

To the many talented people in the marketing, publicity, production editorial, cover design, interior design, special sales, and other departments at Simon & Schuster who worked on this book, thank you for your efforts on this book and all books. What a wonderful impact you have on the world.

Cocoa Bean is the bestest, cutest, cuddliest, most high-energy puppy ever. This book probably would have been written in less time and with less joy without him.

My in-laws are supportive and kind. I am grateful to Naginder Singh, Sarbjit Singh, and Nanda Sugandhi for their constant love and support. I miss my father-in-law, the late Harbhajan Singh, every day.

My sister, Mamta Chugh, is a model of consistency and courage. I love and admire her deeply, through thick and thin. I hope she knows this.

My parents, Suresh and Sudesh Chugh, have taught me what fierce, tenacious, unwavering unconditional love is. Their sacrifices are what have made my life what it is. I will never be able to thank them enough. But if I could, I would.

I know how lucky I am to spend this precious life with my husband, Charnjit (CJ) Singh. Whether laughing on a good day or pushing through on a bad one, we keep building and rebuilding our relationship. I hope he feels a fraction of the support from me that I feel from him. Here is to every day of our next one hundred years together.

And then there are our kids. Hugs, chats, jokes, pep talks, and cheerleading—I have leaned on them throughout the process of writing this book. When we fall down, we get back up: that's what I always tell them. The past few years, that's what they keep modeling for me. There are not enough words or metaphors in the world to express my love, admiration, and gratitude for them. I strive to be the ancestor their descendants will deserve.

Notes

Prologue

1   While my kids are less exposed: Christian Spencer, "Atlanta Fans Celebrate with Cheer Many Consider Racist," *The Hill,* November 3, 2021, https://thehill.com/changing-america/respect/diversity-inclusion/579934-atlanta-fans-celebrate-with-cheer-many-consider.

2   The American Psychological Association recommends: American Psychological Association, "APA Resolution Recommending the Immediate Retirement of American Indian Mascots, Symbols, Images, and Personalities by Schools, Colleges, Universities, Athletic Teams, and Organizations," apa.org, 2005, https://www.apa.org/about/policy/mascots.pdf.

3   The National Congress of American Indians: Ian Record, Ph.D. (2020), https://www.ncai.org/proudtobe.

4   A *New York Times* teacher's resource: Keith Meatto, "Teaching about the Native American Fight for Representation, Repatriation and Recognition," *New York Times,* October 4, 2021, https://www.nytimes.com/2021/10/04/learning/teaching-about-the-native-american-fight-for-representation-repatriation-and-recognition.html.

5   Research by psychologist John Jost: John T. Jost and Mahzarin R. Banaji, "The Role of Stereotyping in System-Justification and the Production of False Consciousness," *Political Psychology*, September 2004, pp. 294–314, https://doi.org/10.4324/9780203505984-17.

6 When we whitewash the past: Merriam-Webster.com, "whitewash," accessed November 29, 2021, https://www.merriam-webster.com/dictionary/whitewash.

7 I am lost in what psychologists call: Leonard Zusne and Warren H. Jones, *Anomalistic Psychology: A Study of Magical Thinking* (New York: Psychology Press Taylor & Francis Group, 2010).

8 Childlike magical thinking: Giora Keinan, "Effects of Stress and Tolerance of Ambiguity on Magical Thinking," *Journal of Personality and Social Psychology* 67, no. 1 (July 1994): 48–55, https://doi.org/10.1037/0022-3514.67.1.48.

9 My friend Jeff Wilser wrote: Jeff Wilser, *The Good News About What's Bad for You . . . the Bad News About What's Good for You* (New York: Flatiron, 2016).

10 One study estimates that between Columbus's arrival: Alexander Koch et al., "Earth System Impacts of the European Arrival and Great Dying in the Americas after 1492," *Quaternary Science Reviews* 207 (March 1, 2019): 13–36, https://doi.org/10.1016/j.quascirev.2018.12.004.

11 As far back as the 1600s: Henry Foley, *Records of the English Province of the Society of Jesus: Historic Facts Illustrative of the Labours and Sufferings of Its Members in the Sixteenth and Seventeenth Centuries* (London: Burns & Oates, 1877).

12 White women got the right to vote: Michael Harriot, "Y'all Tired Yet?" *The Root,* January 8, 2021, https://www.theroot.com/yall-tired-yet-1846003646.

13 In his book *Think Again*: Adam Grant, excerpt from book cover, *Think Again: The Power of Knowing What You Don't Know* (New York: Viking, 2021).

14 The longer we have held knowledge: Karen Becker, "Individual and Organizational Unlearning: Directions for Future Research," *International Journal of Organizational Behaviour* 9, no. 7 (2005): 659–70.

15 Unfortunately, this narrative ignores: U.S. Census Bureau, "Black and Slave Population of the United States from 1790 to 1880," chart, July 8, 2019, Statista, accessed November 29, 2021, https://www.statista.com/statistics/1010169/black-and-slave-population-us-1790-1880/.

16 the genocide of 54 million Native Americans: David Michael Smith, "Counting the Dead: Estimating the Loss of Life in the Indigenous Holocaust 1492–Present," se.edu (University of Houston–Downtown), https://www.se.edu/native-american/wp-content/uploads/sites/49/2019/09/A-NAS-2017-Proceedings-Smith.pdf?bbeml=tp-LoV-wVHX0k6TcA7W

m6g2wQ.jSys0KeQJgUafvsYIdAsKZw.rvHGgn32To02VwLgzvtEx4g .lqjTrZHIjR0WBL7o0wcew3Q.

17 In a study about scientific beliefs, psychologist Deborah Kelemen: Deborah Kelemen, "The Magic of Mechanism: Explanation-Based Instruction on Counterintuitive Concepts in Early Childhood," *Perspectives on Psychological Science* 14, no. 4 (2019): 510–22, https://doi.org/10.1177 /1745691619827011.

18 Kids especially need practice at unlearning: Adam M. Grant, *Think Again* (New York: Viking, 2021).

19 "What would it take—what does it take": Clint Smith, *How the Word Is Passed: A Reckoning with the History of Slavery Across America* (New York: Little, Brown, 2021).

20 Humans—especially from individualistic Western cultures: Joan G. Miller, "Culture and the Development of Everyday Social Explanation," *Journal of Personality and Social Psychology* 46, no. 5 (1984): 961–78, https://doi.org /10.1037/0022-3514.46.5.961.

21 Such behavior is so quintessentially human: Lee Ross, "The Intuitive Psychologist and His Shortcomings: Distortions in the Attribution Process," *Advances in Experimental Social Psychology* (1977): 173–220, https://doi .org/10.1016/s0065-2601(08)60357-3.

22 Our "myside bias" leads us: Keith E. Stanovich, *The Bias That Divides Us: The Science and Politics of Myside Thinking* (Cambridge, MA: MIT Press, 2021).

Chapter 1. See the Problem

1 In the summer of 2020: Robin DiAngelo, *White Fragility: Why It's So Hard for White People to Talk about Racism* (Boston: Beacon Press, 2018).

2 She learned that her new hometown: New-York Historical Society, "The History of Slavery in New York," Slavery in New York Exhibition, http:// www.slaveryinnewyork.org/history.htm.

3 This mental illusion affects everyone: Daniel Kahneman, *Thinking, Fast and Slow* (New York: Farrar, Straus & Giroux, 2013).

4 One Princeton player told: No writer attributed, "Princeton's Quarterback Hits Dartmouth as 'Dirty': News: The Harvard Crimson," *Harvard Crimson,* November 30, 1951, https://www.thecrimson.com/article/1951/11 /30/princetons-quarterback-hits-dartmouth-as-dirty/.

5   In contrast, the Dartmouth coach: C. E. W., "Concerning the Princeton Game: Dartmouth Alumni Magazine: January 1952," *Dartmouth Alumni Magazine,* January 1952, https://archive.dartmouthalumnimagazine.com /article/1952/1/1/concerning-the-princeton-game.

6   which sounds akin to: Amos Tversky and Daniel Kahneman, "Advances in Prospect Theory: Cumulative Representation of Uncertainty," *Journal of Risk and Uncertainty* 5, no. 4 (October 1992): 297–323, https://doi.org /10.1007/bf00122574.

7   With my colleagues Mahzarin Banaji: Dolly Chugh, Max H. Bazerman, and Mahzarin R. Banaji, "Bounded Ethicality as a Psychological Barrier to Recognizing Conflicts of Interest," *Conflicts of Interest* (2005): 74–95, https://doi.org/10.1017/cbo9780511610332.006.

8   which I sometimes refer to as the psychology: Dolly Chugh and Mary C. Kern, "A Dynamic and Cyclical Model of Bounded Ethicality," *Research in Organizational Behavior* 36 (July 2016): 85–100, https://doi.org/10.1016 /j.riob.2016.07.002.

9   These constraints lead to bounded rationality: Herbert A. Simon, *Models of Man: Social and Rational; Mathematical Essays on Rational Human Behavior in Society Setting* (New York: Wiley, 1967).

10 We are also prone to bounded awareness: Max Bazerman and Dolly Chugh, "Bounded Awareness: Focusing Problems in Negotiation," *Frontiers of So-cial Psychology: Negotiations,* ed. L. Thompson (College Park, MD: Psychol-ogy Press, 2005).

11 Researchers have found: Jolanda Jetten and Michael J. Wohl, "The Past as a Determinant of the Present: Historical Continuity, Collective Angst, and Opposition to Immigration," *European Journal of Social Psychology* 42, no. 4 (2011): 442–50, https://doi.org/10.1002/ejsp.865.

12 In these studies, the researchers also measured: Michael J. Wohl and Nyla R. Branscombe, "Group Threat, Collective Angst, and Ingroup Forgiveness for the War in Iraq," *Political Psychology* 30, no. 2 (2009): 193–217, https:// doi.org/10.1111/j.1467-9221.2008.00688.x.

13 Political scientist Diana Mutz: Diana C. Mutz, "Status Threat, Not Eco-nomic Hardship, Explains the 2016 Presidential Vote," *Proceedings of the National Academy of Sciences* 115, no. 19 (April 23, 2018), https://doi.org /10.1073/pnas.1718155115.

14 From their (and others') work, critical race theory: Kimberlé Crenshaw et al., *Critical Race Theory: The Key Writings That Formed the Movement* (New York: New Press, 1996).

15 The teaching of history became front: Lauren Jackson, "What Is Critical

Race Theory?" *New York Times,* July 9, 2021, https://www.nytimes.com/2021/07/09/podcasts/the-daily-newsletter-critical-race-theory.html.

16 Put simply, critical race theory: "What Is Critical Race Theory, and Why Is Everyone Talking about It?" *Columbia News,* July 1, 2021, https://news.columbia.edu/news/what-critical-race-theory-and-why-everyone-talking-about-it-0.

17 For example, the CROWN Act: Britney Pitts, "'Uneasy Lies the Head That Wears a Crown': A Critical Race Analysis of the Crown Act," *Journal of Black Studies* 52, no. 7 (February 2021): 716–35, https://doi.org/10.1177/00219347211021096.

18 Beginning in the 1980s and 1990s: Michelle Alexander, *The New Jim Crow: Mass Incarceration in the Age of Colorblindness* (New York: New Press, 2012), 111.

19 The Fair Sentencing Act: The Caucus blog, "Obama Signs Law Narrowing Cocaine Sentencing Disparities," *New York Times,* August 3, 2010, https://thecaucus.blogs.nytimes.com/2010/08/03/obama-signs-law-narrowing-cocaine-sentencing-disparities.

20 Educator Duncan Koerber: Duncan Koerber, "Truth, Memory, Selectivity: Understanding Historical Work by Writing Personal Histories," *Composition Studies* 41, no. 1 (2013): 51–69, http://www.jstor.org/stable/43501831.

21 Historians Richard Marius and Mel Page explain: Richard Marius and Melvin E. Page, *A Short Guide to Writing About History* (Boston: Pearson, 2015).

22 Loewen shares his findings: James W. Loewen, *Lies My Teacher Told Me: Everything Your American History Textbook Got Wrong* (New York: Simon & Schuster, 2007).

23 In a more recent 2017 study: "Teaching the Hard History of American Slavery," Southern Poverty Law Center, 2017, https://www.splcenter.org/teaching-hard-history-american-slavery.

24 Hasan Kwame Jeffries: Nikita Stewart, "Why Can't We Teach Slavery Right in American Schools?" *New York Times,* August 19, 2019, https://www.nytimes.com/interactive/2019/08/19/magazine/slavery-american-schools.html.

25 One education reporter writes: Stephen Noonoo, "Are History Textbooks Worth Using Anymore? Maybe Not, Some Teachers Say," EdSurge, March 13, 2021, https://www.edsurge.com/news/2020-06-30-are-history-textbooks-worth-using-anymore-maybe-not-say-some-teachers.

26 While whites comprised 20 percent: Aaron O'Neill, "World Population by

Continent 1950–2020," Statista, March 9, 2021, https://www.statista.com
/statistics/997040/world-population-by-continent-1950-2020/.

27 Imagine all three of those things: Trevor Noah, *Born a Crime: Stories from a
South African Childhood* (Berlin: Cornelsen, 2020).

28 Nelson Mandela and other activists: Nelson Mandela, *Long Walk to Freedom: The Autobiography of Nelson Mandela* (London: Little, Brown, 2013).

29 Under apartheid, Jansen explains: Jonathan D. Jansen, *Knowledge in the
Blood: Confronting Race and the Apartheid Past* (Stanford, CA: Stanford
University Press, 2009).

30 "But it is also a defensive knowledge": Ibid., p. 170.

31 Translated into English: Klopjag, "Nie Langer," 859005 Records DK, 2005,
https://open.spotify.com/track/2ux71KdgoFdS6uwIeupUtW?autoplay=true.

32 In her book *Learning from the Germans*: Susan Neiman, *Learning from the
Germans: Race and the Memory of Evil* (New York: Farrar, Straus & Giroux,
2019).

33 In fact, she cowrote an article: Christine H. Leland and Stevie R. Bruzas,
"Becoming Text Analysts: Unpacking Purpose and Perspective," *Language
Arts* 92, no. 1 (2014): 23–35, http://www.jstor.org/stable/24575555.

34 In another coauthored article: Kristal Curry et al., *MidSouth Literacy Journal* 4, no. 2–UAB, https://www.medgrad.uab.edu/, 2019, https://www
.uab.edu/education/mlj/images/Issues/volume-4-issue-2.pdf.

Chapter 2. Dress for the Weather

1 The television industry has stoked: n.d., *Finding Your Roots,* PBS39 WLVT,
accessed December 11, 2021, https://www.wlvt.org/television/national
-shows/finding-your-roots/.

2 Sometimes the guest learns: n.d., *Finding Your Roots,* Season 2 10x60, PBS
International, accessed December 11, 2021, https://pbsinternational.org
programs/finding-your-roots-season-2/.

3 Superstar couple Kyra Sedgwick: Megan Smolenyak, "6 Degrees of Sepa-
ration: Kyra Sedgwick and Kevin Bacon Are Cousins," *HuffPost,* December 7, 2017, https://www.huffpost.com/entry/6-degrees-of-separation-k_b
_900707.

4 Tina Fey learns: n.d., "Tracing Tina Fey's Paternal Line," PBS, 2014,
https://www.pbs.org/weta/finding-your-roots/watch/extras/tracing-tina
-feys-paternal-line.

5 Sarah Jessica Parker hears: *Who Do You Think You Are,* "Sarah Jessica Parker," March 5, 2010.

6 Congressman John Lewis breaks: Rachael Bade, "John Lewis's Tears over Ancestor's Voter Card Stir Emotions in Democratic Caucus," *Washington Post,* June 12, 2019, https://www.washingtonpost.com/powerpost/john-lewiss -tears-over-ancestors-voter-card-stirs-emotions-in-democratic-caucus /2019/06/11/8f568332-8c60-11e9-adf3-f70f78c156e8_story.html.

7 The popularity of *Finding Your Roots:* George Santayana, *The Life of Reason,* vol. 1, *Reason in Common Sense* (New York: Charles Scribner's Sons, 1906).

8 According to one study, in the previous twelve months: Roy Rosenzweig and David P. Thelen, *The Presence of the Past: Popular Uses of History in American Life* (New York: Columbia University Press, 1998).

9 In addition, consumer DNA testing: Antonio Regalado, "2017 Was the Year Consumer DNA Testing Blew Up," *MIT Technology Review,* April 2, 2020, https://www.technologyreview.com/2018/02/12/145676/2017-was -the-year-consumer-dna-testing-blew-up/.

10 In 2014, *Time* magazine published: Gregory Rodriguez, "How Genealogy Became Almost as Popular as Porn," *Time,* May 30, 2014, https://time.com /133811/how-genealogy-became-almost-as-popular-as-porn/.

11 According to the article, genealogy: Alan Farnham, "Who's Your Daddy? Genealogy Becomes $16.B Hobby," ABC News, October 24, 2012, https:// abcnews.go.com/Business/genealogy-hot-hobby-worth-16b-mormons /story?id=17544242.

12 Psychologists argue that one way: Jolanda Jetten and Michael J. Wohl, "The Past as a Determinant of the Present: Historical Continuity, Collective Angst, and Opposition to Immigration," *European Journal of Social Psychology* 42, no. 4 (2012): 443, https://doi.org/10.1002/ejsp.865.

13 For example, my social identities such as American: Henri Tajfel and John C. Turner, "The Social Identity Theory of Intergroup Behavior," *Political Psychology* (2004): 276–93, https://doi.org/10.4324/9780203505984-16.

14 Again, just as with: Gregory R. Gunn and Anne E. Wilson, "Acknowledging the Skeletons in Our Closet," *Personality and Social Psychology Bulletin* 37, no. 11 (June 2011): 1474–87, https://doi.org/10.1177/014616 7211413607.

15 The stories we learn and tell about: James H. Liu and Denis J. Hilton, "How the Past Weighs on the Present: Social Representations of History and Their Role in Identity Politics," *British Journal of Social Psychology* 44, no. 4 (2005): 537–56, https://doi.org/10.1348/014466605x27162.

16 Another study found that popular history: Denis J. Hilton and James H. Liu, "History as the Narrative of a People: From Function to Structure and Content," *Memory Studies* 10, no. 3 (2017): 297–309, https://doi.org /10.1177/1750698017701612.

17 Research shows that nostalgic memories: Constantine Sedikides et al., "Nostalgia: Past, Present, Future," *Current Directions in Psychological Science* 17, no. 5 (2008): 304–7, https://doi.org/10.1111/j.1467-8721.2008 .00595.x.

18 Nostalgia creates a sense: Wijnand A. van Tilburg, Tim Wildschut, and Constantine Sedikides, "Nostalgia's Place among Self-Relevant Emotions," *Cognition and Emotion* 32, no. 4 (2017): 742–59, https://doi.org/10.1080 /02699931.2017.1351331.

19 Our interest in the past is focused on: Roy Rosenzweig and David P. Thelen, *The Presence of the Past: Popular Uses of History in American Life* (New York: Columbia University Press, 1998).

20 Trend research shows that: Patrick Metzger, "The Nostalgia Pendulum: A Rolling 30-Year Cycle of Pop Culture Trends," The Patterning, March 21, 2017, https://thepatterning.com/2017/02/13/the-nostalgia-pendulum-a -rolling-30-year-cycle-of-pop-culture-trends/.

21 We seek nostalgia on vacation: Carolyn Childs, "How Culture and Heritage Tourism Boosts More than a Visitor Economy," MyTravelResearch .com, September 16, 2021, https://www.mytravelresearch.com/culture -and-heritage-tourism-boosts-visitor-economy/.

22 Reynolds later said: Jonathan Ringen, "Ryan Reynolds on 'Deadpool,' Diversity, and the Secrets of Successful Marketing," *Fast Company,* August 4, 2020, https://www.fastcompany.com/90525283/most-creative-people -2020-ryan-reynolds.

23 Our social identities are central: Francesco Massara and Fabio Severino, "Psychological Distance in the Heritage Experience," *Annals of Tourism Research* 42 (2013): 108–29, https://doi.org/10.1016/j.annals.2013.01.005.

24 One study found that the extent: Yaniv Poria, Arie Reichel, and Avital Biran, "Heritage Site Perceptions and Motivations to Visit," *Journal of Travel Research* 44, no. 3 (2006): 318–26, https://doi.org/10.1177 /0047287505279004.

25 We yearn most for personal nostalgia: Michael J. Wohl, Anna Stefaniak, and Anouk Smeekes, "Days of Future Past: Concerns for the Group's Future Prompt Longing for Its Past (and Ways to Reclaim It)," *Current Directions in Psychological Science* 29, no. 5 (June 2020): 481–86, https://doi.org /10.1177/0963721420924766.

26 The students seemed to "bask": Robert B. Cialdini et al., "Basking in Reflected Glory: Three (Football) Field Studies," *Journal of Personality and Social Psychology* 34, no. 3 (September 1976): 366–75, https://doi.org/10.1037/0022-3514.34.3.366.

27 Such basking in reflected glory: Arindam Chakrabarti, "Individual and Collective Pride," *American Philosophical Quarterly* 29, no. 1 (1992): 35–43, http://www.jstor.org/stable/20014396.

28 In a study published in 2018, more than 80 percent: Mark H. White II and Nyla R. Branscombe, "'Patriotism à La Carte': Perceived Legitimacy of Collective Guilt and Collective Pride as Motivators for Political Behavior," *Political Psychology* 40, no. 2 (2018): 223–40, https://doi.org/10.1111/pops.12524.

29 He glances up from a stack: *Finding Your Roots,* "Roots of Freedom," October 14, 2014.

30 "While I don't like that the guy": Ben Affleck, 2015, "After an exhaustive search of my ancestry for 'Finding Your Roots,' it was discovered that one of my distant relatives was an owner of slaves," Facebook, April 21, 2015, https://www.facebook.com/permalink.php?story_fbid=849207928486969&id=147898965284539.

31 The words *guilt* and *shame* are often used interchangeably: June Price Tangney and Ronda L. Dearing, *Shame and Guilt* (New York: Guilford Press, 2004).

32 Guilt is when I feel like I *did*: Paula M. Niedenthal, June Price Tangney, and Igor Gavanski, "'If Only I Weren't' versus 'If Only I Hadn't': Distinguishing Shame and Guilt in Counterfactual Thinking," *Journal of Personality and Social Psychology* 67, no. 4 (November 1994): 585–95, https://doi.org/10.1037/0022-3514.67.4.585.

33 Shame is a particularly: Annette Kämmerer, "The Scientific Underpinnings and Impacts of Shame," *Scientific American,* August 9, 2019, https://www.scientificamerican.com/article/the-scientific-underpinnings-and-impacts-of-shame/.

34 In fact, physiological research even shows that our cardiovascular: Luna Dolezal and Barry Lyons, "Health-Related Shame: An Affective Determinant of Health?" *Medical Humanities* 43, no. 4 (August 2017): 257–63, https://doi.org/10.1136/medhum-2017-011186.

35 Psychologists have found that the positive: Colin Wayne Leach and Atilla Cidam, "When Is Shame Linked to Constructive Approach Orientation? A Meta-Analysis," *Journal of Personality and Social Psychology* 109, no. 6 (2015): 983–1002, https://doi.org/10.1037/pspa0000037.

36 The study participants not only inferred: Rebecca Schaumberg and Samuel Skowronek, "Shame Broadcasts Social Norms: An Experimental Investigation of What People Learn from Others' Shame," *SSRN Electronic Journal,* March 2021, https://doi.org/10.2139/ssrn.3792103.

37 The circumstances that evoke: Brian Lickel et al., "Vicarious Shame and Guilt," *Group Processes & Intergroup Relations* 8, no. 2 (2005): pp. 145–57, https://doi.org/10.1177/1368430205051064.

38 Both collective guilt and collective shame prime: Michael J. Wohl, Nyla R. Branscombe, and Yechiel Klar, "Collective Guilt: Emotional Reactions When One's Group Has Done Wrong or Been Wronged," *European Review of Social Psychology* 17, no. 1 (July 29, 2010): 1–37, https://doi.org/10.1080/10463280600574815.

39 some research finds that group-based guilt: Brian Lickel, Tony Schmader, and M. Spanovic, "Group-Conscious Emotions: The Implications of Others' Wrongdoings for Identity and Relationships," *The Self-Conscious Emotions: Theory and Research* (2007): 351–70.

40 In the animated movie *Rise of the Guardians*: *Rise of the Guardians* (DreamWorks Animation, 2012).

41 In his book *States of Denial*: Stanley Cohen, *States of Denial: Knowing about Atrocities and Suffering* (Cambridge, UK: Polity, 2015).

42 There he shows the same tendency: Anderson Cooper and Gloria Vanderbilt, *The Rainbow Comes and Goes: A Mother and Son on Life, Love, and Loss* (New York: Harper, 2017).

43 This self-threat reflex: Eric D. Knowles et al., "Deny, Distance, or Dismantle? How White Americans Manage a Privileged Identity," *Perspectives on Psychological Science* 9, no. 6 (November 2014): 594–609, https://doi.org/10.1177/1745691614554658.

44 In particular, studies show that helping people: Aleah Burson, Jennifer Crocker, and Dominik Mischkowski, "Two Types of Value-Affirmation," *Social Psychological and Personality Science* 3, no. 4 (January 2012): 510–16, https://doi.org/10.1177/1948550611427773.

45 A reminder of what we care about: Jennifer Crocker, Yu Niiya, and Dominik Mischkowski, "Why Does Writing about Important Values Reduce Defensiveness?" *Psychological Science* 19, no. 7 (2008): 740–47, https://doi.org/10.1111/j.1467-9280.2008.02150.x.

46 Consider this classic study: Geoffrey L. Cohen et al., "Recursive Processes in Self-Affirmation: Intervening to Close the Minority Achievement Gap," *Science* 324, no. 5925 (2009): 400–403, https://doi.org/10.1126/science.1170769.

47 Researcher Geoffrey Cohen explains: Stanford GSB Staff, "The Value of 'Values Affirmation,'" Stanford Graduate School of Business, May 2, 2012, https://www.gsb.stanford.edu/insights/value-values-affirmation.

48 While this finding has been replicated: Akira Miyake et al., "Reducing the Gender Achievement Gap in College Science: A Classroom Study of Values Affirmation," *Science* 330, no. 6008 (2010): 1234–37, https://doi.org /10.1126/science.1195996.

49 Behavioral scientists have even found that prosocial behavior: Claudia R. Schneider and Elke U. Weber, "Motivating Prosocial Behavior by Leveraging Positive Self‚ÄêRegard through Values Affirmation," *Journal of Applied Social Psychology*, November 19, 2021, https://doi.org/10.1111 /jasp.12841.

50 Researchers have extended research on values affirmation: Gregory R. Gunn and Anne E. Wilson, "Acknowledging the Skeletons in Our Closet," *Personality and Social Psychology Bulletin* 37, no. 11 (2011): 1474–87, https://doi .org/10.1177/0146167211413607.

51 Psychologist Daniel Gilbert refers: Timothy D. Wilson and Daniel T. Gilbert, "Affective Forecasting," *Current Directions in Psychological Science* 14, no. 3 (2005): 131–34, https://doi.org/10.1111/j.0963-7214.2005.00355.x.

52 Gilbert and colleagues even find: Daniel T. Gilbert et al., "The Surprising Power of Neighborly Advice," *Science* 323, no. 5921 (2009): 1617–19, https://doi.org/10.1126/science.1166632.

Chapter 3. Embrace Paradox

1 It wasn't until almost one hundred years after the signing: Clarence Lusane, "Analysis: The Emancipation Proclamation Did Not End Slavery. Here's What Did," *Washington Post*, June 28, 2021, https://www.washingtonpost .com/politics/2021/06/25/emancipation-proclamation-did-not-end-slav ery-heres-what-did/.

2 One example is the "binary bias": Matthew Fisher and Frank C. Keil, "The Binary Bias: A Systematic Distortion in the Integration of Information," *Psychological Science* 29, no. 11 (2018): 1846–58, https://doi.org/10.1177 /0956797618792256.

3 In 2021, I wrote a second piece: Dolly Chugh, "Five Ways You Should NOT Honor Juneteenth," *Dear Good People* newsletter, June 18, 2021, https://us19 .campaign-archive.com/?u=f881146700e09f49303435ca1&id=5b98e422f6.

4   In fact, the first African-Americans to integrate: Dolly Chugh, "What's Ju-
    neteenth? A Guide to Celebrating America's Second Independence Day,"
    Forbes, June 26, 2018, https://www.forbes.com/sites/dollychugh/2018/06
    /19/whats-juneteenth-a-guide-to-celebrating-americans-second-indepen
    dence-day/?sh=7d34dc0f6021.

5   "This, our new government, is the first": Alexander H. Stephens, "'Corner-
    stone' Speech," March 21, 1861, from Teaching American History, https://
    teachingamericanhistory.org/document/cornerstone-speech/ (accessed De-
    cember 13, 2021).

6   In his book, *In the Shadow of Statues*: Mitch Landrieu, *In the Shadow of
    Statues: A White Southerner Confronts History* (New York: Penguin Books,
    2019).

7   In their book, *Both/And Thinking*: Wendy Smith and Marianne W. Lewis,
    *Both/And Thinking: Embracing Creative Tensions to Solve Your Toughest Prob-
    lems* (Cambridge, MA: Harvard Business Review Press, 2022).

8   A paradox mindset has been found: Jacob Lomranz and Yael Benyamini,
    "The Ability to Live with Incongruence: Aintegration—the Concept and
    Its Operationalization," *Journal of Adult Development* 23, no. 2 (2015):
    79–92, https://doi.org/10.1007/s10804-015-9223-4.

9   Even better, a paradox mindset can be learned: Lotte S. Lüscher and Mari-
    anne W. Lewis, "Organizational Change and Managerial Sensemaking:
    Working Through Paradox," *Academy of Management Journal* 51, no. 2
    (2008): 221–40, https://doi.org/10.5465/amj.2008.31767217.

10 just by telling people to hold two: Wen Chen, "The Paradoxical Mind and
    Body: Physiological and Neurological Responses to Organizational Para-
    doxes," 2019, https://doi.org/10.32657/10220/49566.

11 The mindset may also have a physiological: Sean T. Hannah et al., "The
    Psychological and Neurological Bases of Leader Self-Complexity and Ef-
    fects on Adaptive Decision-Making," *Journal of Applied Psychology* 98, no. 3
    (2013): 393–411, https://doi.org/10.1037/a0032257.

12 It can enable resilience: Ella Miron-Spektor et al., "Microfoundations of
    Organizational Paradox: The Problem Is How We Think about the Prob-
    lem," *Academy of Management Journal* 61, no. 1 (2018): 26–45, https://doi
    .org/10.5465/amj.2016.0594.

13 lead to more creativity: Ella Miron-Spektor, Francesca Gino, and Linda
    Argote, "Paradoxical Frames and Creative Sparks: Enhancing Individual
    Creativity through Conflict and Integration," *Organizational Behavior
    and Human Decision Processes* 116, no. 2 (2011): 229–40, https://doi.org
    /10.1016/j.obhdp.2011.03.006.

14 The tension of trying to resolve: Russ Vince and Michael Broussine, "Paradox, Defense and Attachment: Accessing and Working with Emotions and Relations Underlying Organizational Change," *Organization Studies* 17, no. 1 (January 1, 1996): 1–21, https://doi.org/10.1177/017084069601700101.

15 that energy can be released for other cognitive and emotional tasks: Ruth Kanfer and Phillip L. Ackerman, "Motivation and Cognitive Abilities: An Integrative/Aptitude-Treatment Interaction Approach to Skill Acquisition," *Journal of Applied Psychology* 74, no. 4 (August 1989): 657–90, https://doi .org/10.1037/0021-9010.74.4.657.

16 Best of all, we develop skills: Naomi B. Rothman and Shimul Melwani, "Feeling Mixed, Ambivalent, and in Flux: The Social Functions of Emotional Complexity for Leaders," *Academy of Management Review* 42, no. 2 (March 2017): 259–82, https://doi.org/10.5465/amr.2014.0355.

17 Eventually this rebuilding effort: Lisa Abraham, "America's 'Top Turnaround Mayor' to Speak at Kent State on Nov. 19," Kent State University, 2020, https://www.kent.edu/kent/news/americas-top-turnaround-mayor -speak-kent-state-nov-19.

18 These positive emotions allow us to navigate: Barbara L. Fredrickson, "The Broaden-and-Build Theory of Positive Emotions," *Philosophical Transactions of the Royal Society of London. Series B: Biological Sciences* 359, no. 1449 (2004): 1367–77, https://doi.org/10.1098/rstb.2004.1512.

Chapter 4. Connect the Dots

1 In 1997 Ina shared: Mary Reinholz, "Through Dolls and Quilts, Keeping Alive Legacy of the Indians," *New York Times*, November 30, 1997, https:// www.nytimes.com/1997/11/30/nyregion/through-dolls-and-quilts-keep ing-alive-legacy-of-the-indians.html.

2 Hannah-Jones pitched the idea: Nikole Hannah-Jones et al., *The 1619 Project: A New Origin Story* (New York: One World, 2021).

3 When the special issue was published: Pierre-Antoine Louis, "'No People Has a Greater Claim to That Flag than Us,'" *New York Times,* September 6, 2019, https://www.nytimes.com/2019/09/06/us/nikole-hannah-jones -interview.html.

4 Hannah-Jones won the 2020 Pulitzer: Multiple contributors, "The 9.8.19 Issue," *New York Times,* 2019, https://www.nytimes.com/issue/magazine /2019/09/05/the-9819-issue.

5   Hannah-Jones writes, "Out of slavery": "The 1619 Project," *New York Times Magazine,* November 9, 2021, https://nyti.ms/37JLWkZ.

6   These questions appeared in a "Black history": Jessica C. Nelson, Glenn Adams, and Phia S. Salter, "The Marley Hypothesis," *Psychological Science* 24, no. 2 (November 2012): 213–18, https://doi.org/10.1177/0956 797612451466.

7   In his iconic 1983 song: "Buffalo Soldier," recorded by Bob Marley and the Wailers, *On Confrontation* (London: Island Records, 1983).

8   In subsequent work, Salter: Courtney M. Bonam et al., "Ignoring History, Denying Racism: Mounting Evidence for the Marley Hypothesis and Epistemologies of Ignorance," *Social Psychological and Personality Science* 10, no. 2 (2018): 257–65, https://doi.org/10.1177/1948550617751583.

9   To study how past actions: B. Keith Payne, Heidi A. Vuletich, and Jazmin L. Brown-Iannuzzi, "Historical Roots of Implicit Bias in Slavery," *Proceedings of the National Academy of Sciences* (2019): 201818816, https://doi.org /10.1073/pnas.1818816116.

10   The test taker groups similar words and images: Brian A. Nosek et al., "Pervasiveness and Correlates of Implicit Attitudes and Stereotypes," *European Review of Social Psychology* 18, no. 1 (2007): 36–88, https://doi.org /10.1080/10463280701489053.

11   Based on 25.8 million IATs: Mahzarin R. Banaji and Anthony G. Greenwald, *Blindspot: Hidden Biases of Good People* (New York: Bantam Books, 2016).

12   On average, we can produce 150 words: National Center for Voice and Speech, "Voice Qualities," Ncvs.org, University of Iowa, http://www.ncvs .org/ncvs/tutorials/voiceprod/tutorial/quality.html.

13   The fluency and automaticity: Shankar Vedantam et al., "The 'Thumbprint of the Culture': Implicit Bias and Police Shootings," NPR, June 6, 2017, https://www.npr.org/transcripts/531578107.

14   Scientists at Stanford University: Nikhil Garg et al., "Word Embeddings Quantify 100 Years of Gender and Ethnic Stereotypes," *Proceedings of the National Academy of Sciences* 115, no. 16 (March 2018), https://doi.org /10.1073/pnas.1720347115.

15   In another study using a related methodology: Aylin Caliskan, Joanna J. Bryson, and Arvind Narayanan, "Semantics Derived Automatically from Language Corpora Contain Human-like Biases," *Science* 356, no. 6334 (2017): 183–86, https://doi.org/10.1126/science.aal4230.

16   For example, housing policy expert: Richard Rothstein, *The Color of Law: A Forgotten History of How Our Government Segregated America* (New York: Liveright, 2018).

17 In his book *She Has Her Mother's Laugh:* Carl Zimmer, *She Has Her Mother's Laugh: The Powers, Perversions, and Potential of Heredity* (New York: Dutton, 2019).

18 In *The Atlantic:* Nathaniel Comfort, "The Weird, Ever-Evolving Story of Your DNA," *The Atlantic,* June 22, 2018, https://www.theatlantic.com /magazine/archive/2018/07/carl-zimmer-she-has-her-mother-s-laugh /561710/.

19 For example, mice were exposed: Brian G. Dias and Kerry J. Ressler, "Parental Olfactory Experience Influences Behavior and Neural Structure in Subsequent Generations," *Nature Neuroscience* 17, no. 1 (January 2013): 89–96, https://doi.org/10.1038/nn.3594.

20 Psychologists Yaacov Trope and Nira Liberman: Yaacov Trope and Nira Liberman, "Construal-Level Theory of Psychological Distance," *Psychological Review* 117, no. 2 (August 2010): 440–63, https://doi.org/10.1037 /a0018963.

21 Psychologists have also found that we put more blame: Ruth H. Warner, Molly J. VanDeursen, and Anna R. Pope, "Temporal Distance as a Determinant of Just World Strategy," *European Journal of Social Psychology* 42, no. 3 (April 2012): 276–84, https://doi.org/10.1002/ejsp.1855.

22 We also tend to feel less emotional: Leaf Van Boven et al., "Feeling Close: Emotional Intensity Reduces Perceived Psychological Distance," *Journal of Personality and Social Psychology* 98, no. 6 (2010): 872–85, https://doi.org /10.1037/a0019262.

23 Our lateral prefrontal: Jiro Okuda et al., "Thinking of the Future and Past: The Roles of the Frontal Pole and the Medial Temporal Lobes," *NeuroImage* 19, no. 4 (2003): 1369–80, https://doi.org/10.1016/s1053 -8119(03)00179-4.

24 cortex and frontopolar cortex: Donna Rose Addis, Alana T. Wong, and Daniel L. Schacter, "Remembering the Past and Imagining the Future: Common and Distinct Neural Substrates during Event Construction and Elaboration," *Neuropsychologia* 45, no. 7 (2007): 1363–77, https://doi.org /10.1016/j.neuropsychologia.2006.10.016.

25 We experience more intense emotion: Eugene M. Caruso, "When the Future Feels Worse than the Past: A Temporal Inconsistency in Moral Judgment," *Journal of Experimental Psychology: General* 139, no. 4 (November 2010): 610–24, https://doi.org/10.1037/a0020757.

26 The bottom line: events in the future: Eugene M. Caruso, Daniel T. Gilbert, and Timothy D. Wilson, "A Wrinkle in Time," *Psychological Science* 19, no. 8 (2008): 796–801, https://doi.org/10.1111/j.1467-9280.2008.02159.x.

27 Because the "future looms larger": Julie Caouette, Michael J. Wohl, and Johanna Peetz, "The Future Weighs Heavier than the Past: Collective Guilt, Perceived Control, and the Influence of Time," *European Journal of Social Psychology* 42, no. 3 (2012): 363–71, https://doi.org/10.1002 /ejsp.1857.

28 This counterintuitive tendency: Melvin J. Lerner, "The Belief in a Just World," in *The Belief in a Just World: Perspectives in Social Psychology* (Boston: Springer, 1980), pp. 9–30, https://doi.org/10.1007/978-1-4899-04 48-5_2.

Chapter 5. Reject Racial Fables

1 Rosa Parks has the second: "Goodbye, Columbus," *Smithsonian,* May 1, 2008, https://www.smithsonianmag.com/history/goodbye-columbus-38785157 /?no-ist.

2 In *The Rebellious Life*: Jeanne Theoharis, *The Rebellious Life of Mrs. Rosa Parks* (Boston: Beacon Press, 2013).

3 We seem wired as humans: David M. Sobel and Natasha Z. Kirkham, "Blickets and Babies: The Development of Causal Reasoning in Toddlers and Infants," *Developmental Psychology* 42, no. 6 (November 2006): 1103–15, https://doi.org/10.1037/0012-1649.42.6.1103.

4 to seek narratives in the world: Brian J. Scholl and Patrice D. Tremoulet, "Perceptual Causality and Animacy," *Trends in Cognitive Sciences* 4, no. 8 (2000): 299–309, https://doi.org/10.1016/s1364-6613(00)01506-0.

5 This transparency of cause and effect appeals: Bernard Weiner, "'Spontaneous' Causal Thinking," *Psychological Bulletin* 97, no. 1 (January 1985): 74–84, https://doi.org/10.1037/0033-2909.97.1.74.

6 Second, the stories "promote": Scott T. Allison and George R. Goethals, "Hero Worship: The Elevation of the Human Spirit," *Journal for the Theory of Social Behaviour* 46, no. 2 (February 2015): 187–210, https://doi.org /10.1111/jtsb.12094.

7 that helps us transcend: Paul K. Piff et al., "Awe, the Small Self, and Prosocial Behavior," *Journal of Personality and Social Psychology* 108, no. 6 (June 2015): 883–99, https://doi.org/10.1037/pspi0000018.

8 Three years after that, still only 36 percent: Elahe Izadi, "Black Lives Matter and America's Long History of Resisting Civil Rights Protesters," *Washington Post,* April 29, 2019, https://www.washingtonpost.com/news/the-fix

/wp/2016/04/19/black-lives-matters-and-americas-long-history-of-resist ing-civil-rights-protesters/.

9 This asymmetric pattern explains: Krishnadev Calamur, "When Mu-hammad Ali Refused to Go to Vietnam," *The Atlantic,* August 31, 2020, https://www.theatlantic.com/news/archive/2016/06/muhammad-ali-viet nam/485717/.

10 The United States had long claimed: Tom Gjelten, "How the Immigration Act of 1965 Inadvertently Changed America," *The Atlantic,* October 2, 2015, https://www.theatlantic.com/politics/archive/2015/10/immigration -act-1965/408409/.

11 A recent census showed that about half: U.S. Census Bureau, QuickFacts, West Windsor Township, Mercer County, New Jersey, July 1, 2019, ac-cessed December 3, 2021, https://www.census.gov/quickfacts/westwind sortownshipmercercountynewjersey

Chapter 6. Take Responsibility

1 As he later wrote in the *Harvard Business Review:* Joseph C. Miller, Michael A. Stanko, and Mariam D. Diallo, "Case Study: When Your Brand Is Rac-ist," *Harvard Business Review,* December 1, 2020, https://hbr.org/2020/11 /case-study-when-your-brand-is-racist.

2 In *Caste*: Isabel Wilkerson, *Caste: The Origins of Our Discontents* (Water-ville, ME: Thorndike Press, 2021).

3 "Our era requires new language": Bila Qureshi, "Isabel Wilkerson Knows That Effective Discussions about Race Require New Language. That's Where 'Caste' Comes in," *Washington Post,* August 13, 2020, https://www .washingtonpost.com/entertainment/books/isabel-wilkerson-knows-that -effective-discussions-about-race-require-new-language-thats-where-caste -comes-in/2020/08/07/7a5b4f06-d81a-11ea-930e-d88518c57dcc_story .html.

4 It's crucial to have a broken: Susan Neiman, *Learning from the Germans: Race and the Memory of Evil* (New York: Farrar, Straus & Giroux, 2019).

5 Similarly, Edward Baptist: Edward E. Baptist, *Half Has Never Been Told: Slavery and the Making of American Capitalism* (New York: Basic Books, 2016).

6 In this book, I mostly avoid using: Bridgette L. Hylton, "Why We Must Stop Referring to Enslaved People as 'Slaves,'" Human Parts Medium,

August 26, 2020, https://humanparts.medium.com/why-we-must-imme
diately-cease-and-desist-referring-to-enslaved-people-as-slaves-85b0ddf
c5f7b.

7 I am affiliated with universities: Mike Roberts, "Let's Stop Saying Master/
Slave," Medium, June 19, 2020, https://medium.com/@mikebroberts/lets
-stop-saying-master-slave-10f1d1bf34df.

8 Research says that apologies matter: Barry R. Schlenker, *Impression Management: The Self-Concept, Social Identity, and Interpersonal Relations* (Mon-
terey, CA: Brooks/Cole, 1980).

9 Effective apologies share several: Roy J. Lewicki, Beth Polin, and Robert B.
Lount, "An Exploration of the Structure of Effective Apologies," *Negotiation and Conflict Management Research* 9, no. 2 (2016): 177–96, https://doi
.org/10.1111/ncmr.12073.

10 Political scientist Melissa Nobles notes: Melissa Nobles, *The Politics of Official Apologies* (New York: Cambridge University Press, 2011), 2.

11 The queen of England offered: Stephen Bates and Henry McDonald,
"Queen Gives Ireland Closest Royals Have Come to Apology for Britain's Actions," *Guardian*, May 19, 2011, https://www.theguardian.com/uk
/2011/may/18/queen-ireland-apology-britains-actions.

12 The Vatican apologized for: Alan Cowell, "After 350 Years, Vatican Says
Galileo Was Right: It Moves," *New York Times*, October 31, 1992, https://
www.nytimes.com/1992/10/31/world/after-350-years-vatican-says-gali
leo-was-right-it-moves.html.

13 and its inaction in the Holocaust: William Drozdiak, "Vatican Apologizes
to Jews," *Washington Post*, March 17, 1998, https://www.washingtonpost
.com/archive/politics/1998/03/17/vatican-apologizes-to-jews/ce5ea6e9
-bd97-4022-b639-288342b63455/.

14 Apologies are a "strong and cheap": Urs Fischbacher and Verena Utikal,
"On the Acceptance of Apologies," *Games and Economic Behavior* 82
(2013): 592–608, https://doi.org/10.1016/j.geb.2013.09.003.

15 For example, the majority of white Americans oppose the idea of reparations: Corey Williams, "AP-Norc Poll: Most Americans Oppose Reparations for Slavery," Associated Press, October 25, 2019, https://apnews.com
/article/va-state-wire-us-news-ap-top-news-slavery-mi-state-wire-76de76e
9870b45d38390cc40e25e8f03.

16 In her 2020 *New York Times Magazine* cover story "What Is Owed": Nikole
Hannah-Jones, "What Is Owed," *New York Times Magazine*, June 24, 2020,
https://www.nytimes.com/interactive/2020/06/24/magazine/reparations
-slavery.html.

17   Even the clichéd forty acres: Sarah McCammon, "The Story behind '40 Acres and a Mule,'" NPR, January 12, 2015, https://www.npr.org/sections /codeswitch/2015/01/12/376781165/the-story-behind-40-acres-and-a-mule.

18   Lynchings . . . no accountability: Alex Fox, "Nearly 2,000 Black Americans Were Lynched during Reconstruction," *Smithsonian,* June 18, 2020, https://www.smithsonianmag.com/smart-news/nearly-2000-black-ameri cans-were-lynched-during-reconstruction-180975120/.

19   Before Ta-Nehisi Coates: Ta-Nehisi Coates, "The Case for Reparations," *The Atlantic,* May 14, 2021, https://www.theatlantic.com/magazine/archive /2014/06/the-case-for-reparations/361631/.

20   The article went viral: "160 Years of Atlantic Stories," *The Atlantic,* November 1, 2017, https://www.theatlantic.com/projects/160-years/.

21   Consider the city of Evanston, Illinois: Julie Bosman, "Chicago Suburb Shapes Reparations for Black Residents: 'It Is the Start,'" *New York Times,* March 22, 2021, https://www.nytimes.com/2021/03/22/us/reparations -evanston-illinois-housing.html.

22   But there is also the possibility: Irene Blanken et al., "A Meta-Analytic Review of Moral Licensing," *Personality and Social Psychology Bulletin* 41, no. 4 (2015): 540–58, https://doi.org/10.1177/0146167215572134.

Chapter 7. Build Grit

1   The English word *internment:* Merriam-Webster.com, s.v. "internment," accessed December 13, 2021, https://www.merriam-webster.com/dictionary /internment.

2   Psychologist Angela Duckworth defines: Angela L. Duckworth et al., "Grit: Perseverance and Passion for Long-Term Goals," *Journal of Personality and Social Psychology* 92, no. 6 (June 2007): 1087–1101, https://doi.org /10.1037/0022-3514.92.6.1087.

3   Researchers define "psychological entitlement": Keith W. Campbell et al., "Psychological Entitlement: Interpersonal Consequences and Validation of a Self-Report Measure," *Journal of Personality Assessment* 83, no. 1 (2004): 29–45, https://doi.org/10.1207/s15327752jpa8301_04.

4   For example, in one study, researchers were able to evoke: Phyllis A. Anastasio and Karen C. Rose, "Beyond Deserving More," *Social Psychological and Personality Science* 5, no. 5 (January 22, 2014): 593–600, https://doi.org /10.1177/1948550613519683.

5 The idea that our country is both exceptional: Seymour Martin Lipset, *American Exceptionalism: A Double-Edged Sword* (New York: Norton, 1996).

6 Psychologist Albert Bandura: Albert Bandura, "Social Cognitive Theory: An Agentic Perspective," *Annual Review of Psychology* 52, no. 1 (February 2001): 1, https://doi.org/10.1146/annurev.psych.52.1.1.

7 An agency mindset consists of: Albert Bandura, "Toward a Psychology of Human Agency: Pathways and Reflections," *Perspectives on Psychological Science* 13, no. 2 (March 29, 2018): 130–36, https://doi.org/10.1177/1745691617699280.

8 The narrator describes a gutting: Oriah Mountain Dreamer, *The Invitation* (London: Element, 2003), 2.

9 The Character Lab website: Angela Duckworth, "Grit," Character Lab, https://characterlab.org/playbooks/grit/.

10 Duckworth and colleagues: Katherine R. Von Culin, Eli Tsukayama, and Angela L. Duckworth, "Unpacking Grit: Motivational Correlates of Perseverance and Passion for Long-Term Goals," *Journal of Positive Psychology* 9, no. 4 (2014): 306–12, https://doi.org/10.1080/17439760.2014.898320.

11 Organizational scholars Amy Wrzesniewski and Jane Dutton: Amy Wrzesniewski and Jane E. Dutton, "Crafting a Job: Revisioning Employees as Active Crafters of Their Work," *Academy of Management Review* 26, no. 2 (April 2001): 179, https://doi.org/10.2307/259118.

Epilogue

1 Recently, one of our kids wrote a poem: Maya Chugh Singh, unpublished poem excerpt, December 2021.

2 "The psychic wound of racism": Carolyn Merchant, "Shades of Darkness: Race and Environmental History," *Environmental History* 8, no. 3 (2003): 380–94, https://doi.org/10.2307/3986200.

3 "And the country itself": Wendell Berry, in *The Hidden Wound* (Berkeley, CA: Counterpoint, 2010), pp. 112, 48.

Index

About the Author

Dr. Dolly Chugh is a Harvard-educated social psychologist at the NYU Stern School of Business, where she is an expert researcher in the psychology of good people and the recipient of many teaching awards. She is best known for her widely viewed TED Talk, her acclaimed first book, *The Person You Mean to Be: How Good People Fight Bias*, and her free, evidence-based, zeitgeisty newsletter, *Dear Good People*.